Help your child read and write

Pearson Education Limited
Edinburgh Gate
Harlow
Essex CM20 2JE
England

© Pearson Education Limited 2007

First published 2007

ISBN 978-1-4058-4024-8

Commissioning Editor: Emma Shackleton
Project Editor: Cheryl Lanyon
Designer: Annette Peppis
Picture Researcher: Jeanette Payne
Cover illustration: Chris Long
Senior Production Controller: Man Fai Lau

Printed in China CTPSC/01

The Publisher's policy is to use paper manufactured from sustainable forests.

contents

Acknowledgements

This book is dedicated to my two wonderful children Esther and Oliver. It is also for Jackie because of her help in reading and commenting on the book, but not least for being a great mum.

My warmest thanks to the parent readers of this book. In particular to Cathy Marchant for her enthusiasm and her comments, and to Mary Reigner-Wilson and Sarah Thacker.

It has been a real pleasure to work with Emma Shackleton and I look forward to our future work. I also want to show my admiration for Cheryl Lanyon's remarkable skills.

I would like to thank Paula Parish for encouraging me to work with Pearson, and to Darin Jewel for our work together.

Before you start

Learning to read and write is not a mechanical exercise, but an organic process. Something organic is natural. And at the heart of organic growth is the environment. This is a good metaphor to describe learning to read and write. Your child can learn to read and write naturally before starting school. All it takes is their innate curiosity, the environment that you create, your interaction, and lots of real reading and writing. Another meaning of organic is the coordination of parts into a single, harmonious whole. Reading is too often treated as a separate thing, but for children to read well they need help with writing, and vice versa.

Although learning to read and write is a natural process, you can't just give children books, paper and pencils and let them get on with it. Your role in the process and your knowledge are vital. In this book I'll advise you on the best ways to support your child and give you the knowledge that you need to do so. You'll find a wealth of ideas to try with your child, but the book is not simply a scheme of activities. Activities alone don't help children learn to read and write.

How do I know my approach works?

The book is built on my knowledge of a range of strategies that help children learn to read and write because, contrary to what you will hear time and again in the media, there is no one simple, magic method. Firstly, the practical evidence: for this you get to meet my two children, Esther and Olly. Both could read and write before they started school. However, this is not just my personal anecdote. Their mother and I systematically collected data in the form of video clips, observation diaries and samples of the children's texts over a ten-year period. I analysed this evidence to better understand our children's development and what helped them. As far as I know, this is the most comprehensive analysis ever undertaken of two children's reading and writing development. I then compared Esther and Olly's development with published case-studies of other children. When I added this to my knowledge of wider research about children's reading and writing development, gained from my professional involvement in Primary and Early Years Education, I felt confident to explain to parents what to expect at the different stages from birth to the age of eleven.

Other evidence came from my work as a teacher. For eight years I taught infants and juniors in inner-city and suburban schools in London, Bradford and Kirklees. I have also worked as a teacher-trainer in Liverpool and Cambridge for ten years, observing hundreds of lessons in a wide range of schools. As a researcher, I have published many articles and books about teaching reading and writing. There can be no doubt that experience of working with children is invaluable in knowing what to expect, as you will know if you have more than one child. With this book you can benefit from my experience and knowledge and avoid some of the pitfalls.

At any of the stages described in this book, don't worry unduly if your child is not showing all the signs of development I include. These are general characteristics for many children but all children develop at their own rate and some will develop more slowly at first.

Two important studies

The book is built throughout on the findings from research, but there are two studies that I particularly want to tell you about in this introduction. They are studies of groups of children who started to read before they started school. In 1966, Dolores Durkin[1] carried out some research in America and published it in a book called *Children who read early*. These were the things that were common to the children's experiences:

✪ Parents read to their children frequently, and also found time to talk with them and answer their questions.

✪ The children more commonly read real books than typical school textbooks or reading-scheme books.

✪ Whole-word learning was used more than letter-sounds for reading, although letter-sounds were used to help writing.

✪ The children were interested in print in their everyday surroundings.

✪ Many of the children were interested in writing as well as reading.

A year later, in 1967, Margaret Clarke[2] published a very similar study in England. She said that although the child's natural abilities were important,

> *The crucial role of the environment, the experiences which the child obtained, their relevance to his interest and the readiness of adults to encourage and to build upon these, should not be underestimated.*

And here are the factors that were common to the children in Margaret Clarke's study:

✪ At least one parent, often the mother, had a deep involvement with their child and their progress.

✪ Parents welcomed the opportunity to talk to their children.

✪ Non-fiction and print in the home and local environment were mentioned as much as the reading of storybooks.

✪ Most of the children used the public library.

✪ Parents would happily break off from other activities and tell their child what words said if the child couldn't work them out independently from the context.

✪ Very few parents taught their children the letter-sounds. If they did, this was to help with writing more than reading. More children learned the letter names first.

✪ The children had a range of strategies for working out difficult words if their parent wasn't available to supply the word.

✪ Many of the children were interested in writing as well as reading.

A taste of what's to come

This book combines all my experience and research with children who learn to read early to give you the best approach to helping your child. Here are some of the things you will find in it:

Wonderful texts to read

Do you recognize this?:

> *In the light of the moon a little egg lay on a leaf.*

It's a quote from one of the most successful books of all time, *The Very Hungry Caterpillar*, by Eric Carle. Children's books are the main ingredient in learning to read. You'll come across old classics and be introduced to radical new writing, such as *Captain Underpants*! There are lists of good books for children's reading at different ages. But, more than this, you will learn *why* the best texts help children learn to read, and how you can use them with your child.

Wonderful texts to write

Children's imagination and creativity when writing is exquisite. You'll refine your code-breaking skills so you can understand and talk about your child's writing. For example, can you decode this?:

My Klone

Try reading it with a Liverpool accent ... Famous football player from Liverpool? OK, now here's a trickier bit of code-breaking for you:

hte e sd dune is cumitow giv sum esdreds to t cids
(See the translation on page 139.)

Hot topics

Teaching grammar does *not* help children learn to read or write, but you need to know a little about the way that language works to be able to help your child. For example, could you accurately define what a sentence is? This book will help you do it. And what is *phonics*: synthetic phonics, analytic phonics or any other kinds of phonics? You'll find out and learn how to use phonics to help your child learn to read and write.

Different ways of thinking

Did you know that good handwriting can help good spelling? You'll see how you can help your child develop good handwriting.

Debates

What do children do in the statutory tests? Why do they have to do them? How can you help? All these questions are answered, and many more.

I hope that when you've read this book, you'll be able to help your child be happy and successful with their reading and writing.

Things you need to know

There are a few conventions used in this book which you need to know about to help you read it. Throughout the book:

Names of letters are in capitals like this:	A	B	C
Sounds the letters make are between slashes like this:	/a/	/b/	/k/

Ages are written like this: 2y 3m (meaning 2 years and 3 months).

> *Direct quotes from books and other sources appear inset and in orange text, like this.*

✪ **The main practical things you can do to help your child learn to read and write are pulled out from the text as feature bullet points that look like this.**

And there's a table of what to expect at each stage of your child's development and things you can do to help at the end of each chapter.

birth to age four

Read a book with a baby, why do that?

When my daughter Esther was three months old I sat her on my lap and cradled her in the crook of my arm. With my hand stretched round her body I could also hold a book so that she could see the pictures and words. My other hand was free to turn pages. It was the first time that I had read a book to her. This reading experience happened every day, sometimes more than once, for a good many years. We did the same with Esther's brother Olly.

A lot of people might think: read a book with a baby, why do that? I did it because I knew the benefits of sharing books with children at all stages in their development. Another reason was that I believed in having high expectations of children's learning. This was not about pushing children ahead of their natural development, but grew from my academic experience and also, by coincidence, from a BBC television series called *Baby Monthly* that was showing at the time of Esther's birth. On one of the programmes, the featured parents met a researcher. During the visit their babies, who were only a few days old, were given dummies that were linked to a computer. Photos of women's faces were shown on the computer screen and these changed each time the baby sucked on their dummy. At only a few days old, the babies were able to recognize their own mother's face and stop sucking the dummy for a fraction longer than normal to hold the computer image! The researcher explained that studies with babies had increasingly turned away from assuming that babies *couldn't* do very much, to having high expectations about what they *could* do and searching for evidence of this. I applied these kinds of high expectations to my own children's development.

The reason I can remember the details and timing of this first reading experience with Esther is because her mum and I kept information in the form of a diary of observations, video footage, samples of drawing and writing (and, later, computer files of the children's writing). As our diary showed, Esther, aged three months, looked at the pictures in the book. This is the very first stage of trying to work out what texts mean. The eyes focus on the lines, shapes, contrasts and colours on the page and in doing so develop connections with the brain. Esther also smiled when the book was opened – she was already enjoying the reading experience! The comfort of being on a parent's lap is, of course, a joy in itself, but the book is an added curiosity which exercises the child's mind.

When we made noises such as animal sounds while reading the book, she smiled again. This was developing the connection between the ears and the brain. She also held her concentration for the whole of the time spent sharing the book. This kind of concentration is different from the other times during the day when a baby might concentrate, for example when drinking milk or watching a mobile hanging above the cot.

From this episode with Esther you can see that learning to read begins almost immediately. Once babies are strong enough to sit up on a lap supported by a parent's arm they are ready to share in the experience of books. As soon as your baby can grasp things they can also benefit by playing with things like plastic bath-books and thick board-books.

Sometimes you should read the text as it is in the book. Your child will enjoy hearing the comforting sounds of your voice and the different way that you speak when reading a book. At other times you may not bother with the words because you just want to share the pictures and maybe point out some of the things that are in the book. At other times you'll do a bit of both.

⭐ **Reading aloud and sharing books with your child are the most important things that you can do to help their reading.**

Sharing books like this can continue for as many years as your child wants you to read aloud to them. After several years of reading independently, I was delighted and slightly surprised that at the age of nine Olly asked me if I would read *Harry Potter and the Half Blood Prince* aloud to him. Mind you, he soon learned that reading in your head is quicker than reading out loud. Before long, he couldn't stand the suspense and had to carry on reading for himself – Dad was left in the slow readers' group!

Nursery rhymes, games and songs

One of the many important reasons for sharing books with your child is that, in time, they will be able to read the words. This is what some people call 'real reading', but it's important not to forget the role that spoken language has in building the foundations for reading. For example, it's now widely recognized that nursery rhymes play an important part in early learning. One element of this is their contribution to children's *phonological awareness*. This is awareness of the sounds that make up words, which is an important part of learning to read (see Chapter 2). However, nursery rhymes offer a wide range of other learning opportunities, such as music and movement awareness, cultural and moral understanding, learning numbers and letters, the social enjoyment of chanting rhymes, and so on.

✪ **Enjoy as many nursery rhymes and songs with your child as possible. The rhythms, sounds, meanings, actions, structures and music of these are building important foundations for your child's reading.**

It's understandable that people sometimes dismiss nursery rhymes as merely a charming aspect of children's development, but their significance has been recognized by researchers for some time. In the 1950s, Iona and Peter Opie were among the first researchers to see children's language as being worth serious study. Their work was published in three key books: *The Oxford Dictionary of Nursery Rhymes*,[1] *Children's Games in Street and Playground* and *The Lore and Language of Schoolchildren*. In *The Oxford Dictionary of Nursery Rhymes*, the Opies explain the origins of hundreds of nursery rhymes. Let's take a well-known favourite:

Ring-a-ring o' roses
A pocket full of posies,
A-tishoo! A-tishoo!
We all fall down.

Although nowadays we all know the familiar words to this nursery rhyme, it wasn't always the case. The Opies tell us that before 1898 a collector of rhymes called Lady Gomme found twelve versions of the words, with only one being similar to the one we know now. For example, in New Bedford, Massachusetts, during 1790 they sang:

Round the ring of roses,
Pots full of posies,
The one who stoops last
Shall tell whom she loves best.[1]

There's a common idea that *Ring-a-Ring o' Roses* refers to the Great Plague in England. People say that a rosy rash was a symptom of the plague and that posies of herbs were carried as protection. The sneezing was a final, fatal symptom, and 'all fall down' was exactly what happened. The evidence the Opies found led them to dispute this idea. The foreign and nineteenth-century versions seemed to show that the 'fall' was originally a curtsy or other gracious bending movement that was part of a dramatic singing game. There was also often a second verse in which children got to their feet, which also fitted the idea of a singing game:

The cows are in the meadow
Lying fast asleep,
A-tishoo! A-tishoo!
We all get up again.[2]

In more recent times playgroups and nurseries have added a verse in which the children get to their feet:

Down at the bottom of the deep blue sea,
Catching fishes for my tea.
With a one, and a two, and a three!

Here's an example of Esther's experience with a nursery rhyme. When she was two years and four months old (2y 4m), she went to a nursery for two mornings a week. One day I realized that as Esther was singing *Baa Baa Black Sheep* to herself she had added a second verse:

> *Want to make a jumper, want to make a skirt,*
> *(made up words and sounds)...a woolly shirt.*
> *Thank you to the master, thank you to the dame,*
> *Thank you to the little boy who lives down the lane.*

At the point where she couldn't remember the words she just made something up: this shows the way children bring creativity to their learning. When I spoke to one of the nursery nurses she explained that they added the following verses:

> *One to make a blanket,*
> *One to make a skirt,*
> *One to make the little boy*
> *a woolly, woolly shirt.*
>
> *'Thank you,' said the master,*
> *'Thank you,' said the dame,*
> *'Thank you,' said the little boy,*
> *who lives down the lane.*

As with any aspect of learning, you can see from this example that the child's role is not just a passive one.

What is reading?

This is a fundamental question when considering the way that you help your child. I particularly like this definition:

> *Reading is the process of* understanding *speech written down. The goal is to gain access to* meaning.[3]

The two important words in this definition are 'understanding' and 'meaning'. To explain further, let's take an example. Can you read this?:

Eens op een tijd

Even if you don't recognize the words, can you sound them out? When you sounded them out, was that reading? Not according to my definition because there was no understanding of the meaning. Just so you know, 'Eens op een tijd' means 'Once upon a time' in Dutch, according to the internet text translator tool I used! You can see that it's possible to decode the sound of words without understanding. I have worked with children who've been able to read words, but when you ask them about what they've just read they don't know because they've been too focused on decoding using the sounds. Another example of reading without understanding the meaning is just before you go to sleep. Have you ever read a book as you were getting tired and realized that you haven't taken in the last sentence, paragraph or even a whole page?

Children actively try to understand everything in their life. As part of this they search for the meanings of texts and pictures. Although at the beginning children can't fully understand print or decode words, most educators still regard this as an early form of reading. This is once again about high expectations, but is also due to the fact that learning to read is an *organic* or *developmental process*, not something that suddenly begins at one point in time.

✪ **Try to remember that at the heart of everything you do to help your child is the search for *meaning*.**

Wonderful books – birth to age four

The particular books that you and your child choose to read are a vital part of their learning. There are two main kinds of books for children who are learning to read. *Trade books* are the children's books that you can buy in normal bookshops and online and they offer a fantastic range of reading material. They are written by authors who have a desire to communicate their ideas to children in a way that they'll enjoy and think about. *Reading scheme books* are more often written by consultants who work for companies that specialize in classroom teaching resources. You do *not* need to use reading scheme books to help your child to read. In fact, there are many things to be learned from trade books that are simply not present in reading scheme books. Most school infant departments use a mixture of reading scheme and trade books so your child will still benefit from the different advantages that scheme books offer. There are major differences in the kinds of books that are likely to benefit children from birth to two years old and those that will benefit the two- to four-year-olds.

Books from birth to two years old

The wonderful books that you can share with your child are one of the joys of helping them learn to read. But which ones do you choose? You need to learn something about the ways that different kinds of books can help your child's reading. Even for babies there are some books that are particularly helpful.

✪ **The right choice of books will help your child's reading.**
✪ **It's really worthwhile to develop a set of principles to apply when you and your child are selecting books. You'll find guidance on both of these points below.**

I *could* write a list of books and tell you to buy them because they are good. But choosing books should always be a matter of personal preference, so although I'll recommend specific books, it's better if I can help you to understand *why* they are good, rather than have you think that they are the only ones worth buying. That way, you'll have a set of principles to apply when developing your own and your child's preferences for favourite texts. Another reason to have a good idea of the principles of how to select a book is that many children's books go out of print quite quickly unless they are extremely successful, so recommendations may be of short-lived value.

Let's start with some books for the very first years of life. A book called *Where is my home?* was one of my children's favourites. The text was simple:

> *Page 1: I'm lost! Please can you help me find my home?*
> *Page 2: Is it in a flowerpot?*

Page 3: Is it in a sunflower?
Page 4: Is it in a honey jar?
Page 5: Is it in a watering can?
Page 6: Perhaps a nest?
Page 7: Maybe a toadstool...
Page 8: NO!
Page 9: ... a hive? ... YES!

Looks pretty unremarkable doesn't it? Well, let me tell you more. The book is made of cloth and has an interesting texture like the soft toys that children enjoy. The

A page from *Where is my home?*, a Sunshine Garden Activity Book sold by the Boots Company PLC

picture above shows the cloth bumble bee with a smiling human face that features in the book. The bee is attached to the front of the book with a Velcro® patch. The book can only be opened by undoing a simple cloth strip which is secured with more Velcro®. So the secrets of the book literally have to be unlocked. The satisfaction of releasing the Velcro® is accompanied by an intriguing ripping sound as you open the book.

The playfulness of the book is first revealed on page two. There's a hole in the top of the picture of a flowerpot for the bee to be put in... and taken out...and put in...and taken out. Then on all the other pages, showing pictures of different possible homes, there are similar holes to try. Physically putting the main character, the bee, into different homes really engages the child's interest, just like toys which encourage children to post objects through holes.

The book is built around a useful and accurate piece of knowledge: that bees live in hives not in flowerpots, sunflowers, honey jars and so on. Some books for young children neglect the opportunity to communicate accurate knowledge as well as to be entertaining. The pictures in *Where is my home?* are simple and comforting, with bold colours – almost cartoon-like. They link strongly with the text. The structure of the text works very well. A problem is posed on the first page and is resolved on the last page. The repetition of the words 'Is it in...?' helps children to hear and remember words that they will one day speak. Repetition is a very important feature of all good picture books, but it must be set in a meaningful and engaging context. In this book it is. What's more, the repetition is changed on page six from 'Is it in' to 'Perhaps a nest' to avoid becoming boring. My only criticism is that the text on page nine perhaps should have said 'Do I live in a hive?' in order to avoid the slight confusion that the ellipsis (three dots) causes although, having said that, I like the idea of using varied and meaningful punctuation. I would also add that the word 'bee' not appearing in the book misses a trick. The last page could even have been 'Do bees live in hives?' although this would change what is good use of the more personal first person 'I' used at the start of the book.

Here's a summary of why this book is good for babies:

✪ The book is built on a game to play and a puzzle to solve but maintains a clear narrative.

✪ Putting the bee in the pockets is fun.

✪ The pictures are eye-catching and link well with the text.

✪ The knowledge portrayed in the book is important.

✪ The structure of the book is satisfying.

✪ The use of language, including repetition, builds on phrases from spoken interaction and is engaging.

✪ The book is tactile and durable.

The table on the right shows more types of books that would be good for your child's collection.

Books for children from birth to two

Type of book	Example
A lift-the-flap book	*Is that an elephant over there?* Written by Rebecca Elgar
One nursery rhyme in a book	*Humpty Dumpty.* Illustrated by Tracey Moroney
Plastic bath-book	*On the Water,* by Mark Burgess
Television tie-in	*Teletubbies: The Flying Toast,* adapted by Andrew Davenport
A counting book	*How Many Bugs in a Box?,* by David A. Carter
A classic	*Cat on the Mat,* by Brian Wildesmith
An information book	*Diggers and Dumpers,* by Nicola Tuxworth
Play rhymes	*Round and Round the Garden. Play rhymes for young children,* by Ian Beck and Sarah Williams
An alphabet book (an old book from my childhood)	*ABC,* a Ladybird book illustrated by Gerald Witcomb
A book with a favourite character	*Spot at the Carnival,* by Eric Hill

Why is it good?	Any limitations?	By same author
Animals are hidden behind flaps. Your child can pull down flaps and you/your child can say the name of the animal.	Lack of narrative. Just because a book has flaps or pop-ups, doesn't mean that it's good.	*Can You Find Boo?: In the Antarctic*
You can make links from spoken/sung nursery rhymes to printed ones.	Shouldn't replace simply singing nursery rhymes with your child.	*Classic Treasury of Nursery Songs and Rhymes*
You can see different pictures of things on the water by turning pages. Book will survive the bath.	Very limited narrative.	*The Good Egg Yolk Book*
Features the Teletubbies, from a favourite programme.	Simplification of TV script so narrative a bit clumsy.	N/A
Brilliant pop-up effects. Imaginative book design including wonderful colours and range of 'bugs'.	Likely to be damaged by youngest children.	*How Many Bugs in a Box?* 2006 version
Using an everyday phrase, Wildesmith creates an absolute gem. Visually stunning and structurally perfect miniature.	None	*Brian Wildesmith's Animals to Count*
Photographs show big toys and a mixture of girls and boys from different ethnic origins. Uses first person and includes onomatopoeia, like 'Splat', 'Brrrm! Brrrm!'	Slightly too much information in limited structure.	*Splish, Splash*
Tape of music available. Shows actions in little 'story-board' at bottom of each rhyme. Includes some less well-known examples.	Just occasionally it's difficult to fit the actions with the rhyme.	*Round and Round the Garden. Play rhymes for young children* (1999)
Familiar pictures clearly linking with each letter of the alphabet. Old books look so different – this is interesting for children from age three onwards.	A little unimaginative compared to alphabet books that are available now.	N/A
The images of Spot the dog engage children from a very young age. Simple, cartoon-like, yet full of character.	Doesn't really stretch children's thinking.	*Spot's Noisy Toy Box*

My explanation, and particularly the list of why *Where is my home?* is a good book, can guide your own choices when it comes to selecting books for your baby. However, it's only one kind of book so you also need advice on a selection of other books that might be good for babies, and why they are good. The table on the previous page gives examples of books that my own children loved from each type, and the most recent publications by the same authors. You should not, though, feel you must buy the specific books I recommend. Buying the *range* of different types of books, guided by these suggestions, is the key.

Books for two- to four-year-olds

Let's now turn to children who are aged two to four. These children are lucky because they'll be able to read the best children's picture book ever written (in my opinion!). Eric Carle's book *The Very Hungry Caterpillar* is an absolute classic. Here's what the journalist Kate Taylor had to say about it:

> *I have just finished making a radio programme about a book. Thirty-five years old and just 224 words long, it has nevertheless sold a copy somewhere in the world every single minute since it was first published. It has been translated into more than 30 different languages, from Swahili to Catalan, worldwide sales top the 20m mark, and in one edition, if not several, is a constant presence on the UK's bestseller lists. 'It is one of our most successful books of all time,' says Francesca Dow, managing director of Puffin Books. 'It's a publisher's dream and we are very lucky to have it.'*[4]

More important than its overwhelming success is the question of why it is such a good book for helping children learn to read. The book is about what are sometimes called 'minibeasts': in this case, a caterpillar. Children are curious about all animals. You see it when they squat down, having spotted something moving, and gaze for minutes at the slow progress of a snail, a woodlouse, a spider or a centipede. But this is no ordinary caterpillar because, although he does munch his way through nice green leaves, he also tries chocolate cake, ice-cream, pickle, Swiss cheese, salami, a lollipop, some cherry pie, a sausage, a cupcake and one slice of watermelon. He then gets a stomachache! Children learn about the life-cycle of a caterpillar. They also learn that some foods are more healthy than others. Quite a few of the foods the caterpillar eats may well be unfamiliar to children, so this can generate discussion about the different kinds of foods that people eat.

Carle's brilliance as an illustrator is shown in his original use of collage and paint techniques to bring his creation to life (many of the best picture-book authors started their career as artists). The illustrations are accompanied by text which is in a different place on every page. You can use this to see if your child can point to the text, and its starting point, on each page (see more about the importance of this on page 38).

The structure of the book mirrors the life-cycle: it starts with an egg:

In the light of the moon a little egg lay on a leaf.

The egg hatches; the caterpillar has to eat to grow; at the end of his life he forms a cocoon; then finally 'a beautiful butterfly' emerges. One of the master-strokes is this section of the book:

On Monday he ate through one apple. But he was still hungry.
On Tuesday he ate through two pears. But he was still hungry.
On Wednesday he ate through three plums. But he was still hungry.
On Thursday he ate through four strawberries. But he was still hungry.
On Friday he ate through five oranges. But he was still hungry.

As well as enjoying sticking their fingers through the hole in the fruits on each page of this section, children are getting an early lesson in counting. Encouraging them to count the fruits will help them learn to match a spoken number with the pictures of fruits, something known as one-to-one correspondence, which is an important early precursor to counting and reading.

It's hard to believe that Eric Carle's idea to use real holes through the foods the caterpillar eats, and different sizes of cut-away pages to accentuate the eating through the week, was so revolutionary when you think about all the pop-up books and other kinds of book technology that exist today. Not only do children enjoy the holes in the book but they also want to know why they are there.

The use of language in the book is inspiring. Engaging repetition of key phrases is mixed with varied sentences which propel the narrative. The use of the word 'cocoon' is significant. Carle uses the proper scientific term and does not try to 'dumb down' or use an alternative phrase. This challenges children and begs them to ask, 'What's a cocoon?' The answer clearly helps their scientific knowledge.

The table on the right shows more types of books that will particularly appeal to children aged between two and four. But first, here's a summary of why *The Very Hungry Caterpillar* is so good for helping children learn to read, and learn in general:

✪ Children are interested in the topic of the book.

✪ The main character is appealing.

Books for children aged two to four

Type of book	Example
A classic	*A Dark, Dark Tale*, by Ruth Brown
Based on a game	*What's the Time Mr Wolf?*, by Colin Hawkins
A counting book	*One Rich Rajah*, by Sheila and Charles Front
A song book	*Game-Songs With Prof Dogg's Troupe*
Books designed explicitly to help reading	*Inside Outside Upside Down*, by Stan and Jan Berenstein
Innovative book technology	*Ketchup On Your Corn-Flakes*, by Nick Sharratt
A more sophisticated alphabet book	*I Spy: An Alphabet in Art*, by Lucy Micklethwaite
An information book	*See How They Grow: Mouse*, written by Angela Royston with photographs by Barrie Watts
An information book with innovative technology	*Fruit* (First Discovery), translated by S. Matthews

Why is it good?	Any limitations?	By same author
Imaginative use of repetition to take children on a spooky journey from a 'dark dark moor' to a mouse in a box.	Only just avoids being too repetitive.	*Night-Time Tale*
Familiar game and familiar character of the wolf put into lively new context. Helps with telling the time.	Game structure means that the book is repetitive in a way which reduces interest in re-readings.	*Witch Pigs*
India and Indian characters/animals used as backdrop.	Only counts to 10.	*Never Say Macbeth*
Easy enjoyable songs with fun actions. Always good to let children see links between known songs and text (and music).	Many parents won't know the songs but there is a tape to go with the book.	*Game-Songs With Prof Dogg's Troupe,* 2001 edition
Simple, repetitive vocabulary used in an imaginative way. Same style as *The Cat in the Hat* books which are similarly clever at developing skills.	Not as interesting as real storybooks like the ones discussed in this chapter.	*The Berenstein Bears and the Excuse Note*
Card pages cut in half allow you to combine text and pictures in amusing ways: 'Do you like a woolly hat on your apple pie?'	No narrative.	*Don't Put Your Finger in the Jelly Nelly*
Uses I-spy game to encourage children to find objects beginning with the appropriate letter in a different famous painting for each letter. Develops alphabet skills and appreciation of art.	No narrative.	*Colours: A First Art Book*
Very clear and detailed photographs with beautiful layout. Written from perspective of mouse which links with children's familiarity with and love of story.	May not be an interesting subject for some children.	*Glass: Let's Look at Marbles*
A magical series by Moonlight Publishing, who include acetate overlay pages to vary the detail of the illustrations. Wonderful language, remarkably in that it was translated from French.	None	Unknown

✪ The artwork is original and eye-catching for children.

✪ The life-cycle and healthy eating are important things to learn about.

✪ Children love the holes in the pages which are an integral part of the story, not just added for effect.

✪ The satisfying structure mirrors the book's main theme.

✪ Children learn about the days of the week and about counting.

✪ Repetitive language is used naturally.

It's important to remember that really good picture books appeal to children of a wide range of ages, and the best ones should even have something of interest to adults!

Top Ten things to think about for children's books

The list below brings together all the information you've read so far in two checklists of my Top Ten things to think about when you select books for your child.

Age: birth to two

1 Is the subject of the book interesting?

2 In what ways does the book link with your child's world and offer new perspectives?

3 What kind of visual, auditory and tactile experience will the book give?

4 Does the book encourage playfulness?

5 Do the pictures support the text and are they artistically original and memorable?

6 Is the book durable?

7 What kind of knowledge might the child acquire by reading the book?

8 Is the structure of the book effective and satisfying?

9 Is the author's use of language imaginative?

10 Will the character(s) appeal to your child?

Age: two to four

1 Is the subject of the book one that will interest your child?

2 In what ways does the book link with your child's world and offer new perspectives?

3 Is the narrative strong?

4 Does the book involve play and games?

5 Do the pictures support the text and are they artistically original and memorable?

6 Are the amount and level of text appropriate for the age of your child?

7 What kind of knowledge might the child acquire by reading the book?

8 Is the structure of the book effective and satisfying?

9 Is repetitive and realistic language used naturally?

10 Will the book support your child's learning?

✪ In general, I recommend that book choices should sometimes be made by your child and sometimes by you.

✪ Don't worry if children sometimes select books that seem to you to be a bit difficult. From time to time it's more important to encourage them to develop their own preferences, rather than censoring or overruling them. Your selection of books will complement your child's, leading to a richer experience overall.

How to read with your child

✪ Reading with your child should be a comfortable experience for all concerned. Let your child take the lead and read wherever and whenever they feel like it.

A warm spot on a settee is as good a place as any for reading, but if they want to read on the grass in the garden or the park, fair enough. You may want to join them on the carpet as they lie on their tummy. There's no particular time that is better than another for reading – any time of day is fine. However, reading before bedtime can be a particularly enjoyable and comforting experience. Don Holdaway[5] thought that bedtime reading was so important that in 1979 he developed a system called the 'shared book experience'. His approach used enlarged-print books, or 'big books', as a way to emulate the benefits of bedtime reading in school. He called this the 'pre-school bedtime-story learning cycle'. These steps show what happens when you read with your child, and that Don Holdaway reproduced in the classroom:

1   The parent introduces a new story. The child is curious so they ask questions and predict the things that are likely to happen next.
2   If the child likes the story, they ask for it to be re-read immediately and/or later on. They participate more each time they hear the story. The number of questions they ask increases.
3   If the book is stored somewhere accessible, they use it later to play at reading and to re-enact the story independently which gives them additional satisfaction.
4   Further re-readings result in the child becoming more familiar with the book.
5   Play-reading and re-enactment become closer to the language of the text.
6   The concepts, language and attributes of the story are extended into play.
7   The book may become an 'old favourite' and/or attention turns to the beginning of the cycle with a new book.

When you read books to your child, it helps if your voice communicates enthusiasm for the text to help make the meaning clear and the story interesting.

✪ **It's a good idea to animate books with varied speech sounds and rhythms; add accents and other dramatic effects if you can.**

Don't worry, you don't have to be Sir Laurence Olivier or Dame Judi Dench to read aloud well, although if you enjoy doing dramatic turns children often like it! Whenever possible, you should read the words of the text faithfully. This means that on each reading your child will hear the same words and can begin to know the text from memory. The only time I make an exception to this is if the text is too difficult or too long. For example, some film tie-in texts, such as Disney books, are too long which makes them difficult to read aloud successfully. On these occasions I simplify the text (this isn't necessary for any of the books I've recommended in this chapter).

Playing at reading

One of the important ways that young children learn is through play. This applies to reading and writing just as much as to other areas of learning. Sharing books with your child leads to them play-reading with the books independently. Playing games such as 'I-spy', picture/word lotto and others is a more structured form of play which helps with literacy. Children will also engage in role-play.

Esther and Olly were very keen on playing 'shop' when they were at this stage. This involved them taking nearly all the cereal packets, tin cans, drinks, crisps and basically anything that they could get their hands on in the kitchen, and setting them up as a shop somewhere else. I have to admit that this was a stern test of our belief in learning from print – the thought of returning all the food to the right places was not particularly appealing! The wide range of learning that takes place in this kind of role-play scenario is important, and can be enhanced if you join in. If you take on the role of a customer – pay using real money; ask for some things that your child will really have to search hard for by trying to read the labels – you'll be helping them to learn more about reading and lots of other life skills.

Let's look at how Olly played at reading. Early one morning when he was 2y 5m he arranged a mixture of books and children's magazines in a neat semi-circle around him on his bedroom floor. He started singing his largely made-up version of the *Postman Pat* song from the children's TV programme while he selected from the different texts that he had in front of him. His play on this occasion involved choosing some texts from his shelves, organising them on the floor in front of him, browsing through them, and singing a song inspired by one of them.

On another occasion, when he was the same age, he sat at the kitchen table flicking though the *I Spy Book of Cars*. His intense interest in playing with toy cars was a precursor to his interest in books with pictures of cars in them. As he was flicking through the pages he said, 'That's like grandma's car!' In general, he tended to play at reading more when he was alone than if there was an adult in the room. If there was an adult present he would frequently ask them to read his chosen book.

✪ **It can work well if sometimes you deliberately engineer situations where your child has to read independently.**

Amazing memories

From the age of about two-and-a-half onwards, children will begin to remember the words from familiar picture books. A year or so later, this memory of the words may be matched with the printed text to support their decoding of words. Let's look at an example.

When Olly was 2y 10m, his mum videoed him sharing *The Very Hungry Caterpillar* with me and his sister just before he went to bed. Even before the reading began, his imagination and natural curiosity showed when he created a game to play using the inside title page. You can see in the picture of the page shown opposite that the bottom half has lots of multicoloured dots in seven rows stretching across the page. Olly always liked to choose one of them:

OLLY: **Purple.**

ESTHER: **I'm going to choose one...where's purple, dad?**

DAD: **There's purple.**

ESTHER: **I'm gonna have that colour.**

DAD: **Turquoise, I think that is.**

ESTHER: **Yeah!**

OLLY: **I'm gonna ...white ... where's white gone?**

DAD: **There isn't a white is there? Never mind [I try to turn the page to the first page of the story but Olly excitedly stops me].**

OLLY: **I'm gonna choose one!**

THE VERY
HUNGRY
CATERPILLAR

by Eric Carle

PUFFIN BOOKS

**Title page from *The Very Hungry Caterpillar*, by Eric Carle,
Puffin Books in association with Hamish Hamilton**

In this quite natural way Olly was learning about colours. Next he started
'reading' the book. He couldn't read the words so he used his memory of
the text – and what an amazing memory children have for stories. Below
you can compare some of the text of the book with how Olly read it;
remember that Olly is not decoding words yet, just using his memory and
the prompts provided by the pictures.

Book text

In the light of the moon a little egg
lay on a leaf.
One Sunday morning the warm sun
came up and -- pop! -- out of the
egg came a tiny and very hungry
caterpillar.
He started to look for some food.
On Monday he ate through one
apple. But he was still hungry.

Olly's reading

**OLLY: The light of the moon a little
egg lay on a leaf...
one Sunday morning the warm sun
came and POP out of the egg, tiny
and very hungry caterpillar;**

**started to look for some food.
One day**
DAD: Monday
**OLLY: Monday he ate through
one apple but he was still hungry.**

Book text	Olly's reading
On Tuesday he ate through two pears, but he was still hungry. (...)	**On Friday** DAD: **Tuesday** OLLY: **Tuesday he ate through one, two pears but he was still hungry. Getting full. (...)**
On Friday (...)	**On Tuesday** DAD: **Friday** OLLY: **Friday** **(...)**
On Saturday he ate through one piece of chocolate cake, one ice-cream cone, one pickle, one slice of Swiss cheese, one slice of salami, one lollipop, one piece of cherry pie, one sausage, one cupcake, and one slice of watermelon. That night he had a stomachache!	OLLY: **Saturday he ate through one piece of chocolate cake [points to each food in turn], one ice-cream, one pickle, one slice Swiss cheese, one salami, one lollipop, one cherry pie, one sausage, one cupcake, one watermelon, has... had a stomachache [pointing to poorly caterpillar].**

The struggle with the days of the week in the extract above is fascinating. Olly knew that the story featured days of the week but he couldn't remember which day was which, and he couldn't decode the words, so he started by guessing 'Friday'. Later he realized that you can't have Friday for all the days of the week but, just at the wrong moment, as the story finally reached Friday he tried 'Tuesday'! Remembering the sequence of the days of the week is hard for children because they seem to be a random set of words – much harder to memorize than a strong storyline. Notice also Olly's comment that the caterpillar was getting full. This showed he was thinking about the story as a whole as well as the words.

Olly's reading also shows other areas of learning. You could not have a clearer example of a book teaching a child how to count. Olly counted aloud, starting from one, each time he came to a number in the story: 'Tuesday he ate through one, two pears but he was still hungry'. He was confident to count up to four but needed to be told the number five. The part where Olly reads the long list of foods for Saturday shows children's impressive memory capacity.

Lists like these help with the development of one-to-one correspondence. Olly's reading continued up to the final part where the language becomes more complicated. He was getting tired by this point and wanted to finish drinking his milk, so I finished reading the book for him.

To sum up, Olly had only been able to talk for about a year and yet had memorized, almost word-for-word, at least 75 per cent of the story. This memory for the language of stories is called 'talking like a book'.

✪ **Encourage 'reading' books from memory, or 'talking like a book', because it is laying the foundations for decoding words.**

Every picture tells a story

Pictures are an integral part of stories for young children (and for adults in graphic texts). In some of the very simplest picture books they provide a straightforward link with the words. In these early books children use the illustrations to remind them about the story. For more complex books the pictures only provide a limited number of *direct* clues to the text. The links in these books are much more intriguing and subtle; the pictures often tell their own stories, a bit like additional plot lines in adult books. The best picture books encourage children to examine and re-examine the pictures, thinking about the storylines that they portray.

✪ **Always be willing to discuss pictures in books and encourage your child to talk about them.**

Let's have a look at an example of a picture book and the way that children respond to the pictures. *Lily Takes a Walk* is a lovely book, written and illustrated by Satoshi Kitamura. The text goes like this:

Lily likes going for walks with her dog, Nicky.

(...)

Lily is never scared because
Nicky is there with her.

Cover of *Lily Takes a Walk*, by Satoshi Kitamura, Catnip Publishing

The book then book carries on to talk about what they do on their walks: very ordinary, seemingly mundane things. They do some shopping, they look at the stars coming out, they walk past neighbours' houses and see familiar people in the lit windows. They walk over the canal and then see the welcome sight of home, where Lily's mother and father are waiting. They go to bed and Lily says goodnight to Nicky.

There could be no better way of revealing how important the pictures are to a book like this than seeing the words on their own, as above. The text has a lean quality to it which leaves much to the imagination; arguably, it reads like poetry. Yet without the pictures much of the magic of the book is lost. At a straightforward level the pictures provide the urban scene for Lily's walk with her dog.
The sub-plot is revealed by the view that Nicky the dog sees. This transforms the mundane landscape into one filled with scary faces

She stops by the bridge to say goodnight
to the gulls and the ducks on the canal.

Image from _Lily Takes a Walk_, by Satoshi Kitamura, Catnip Publishing

at every turn, such as vampires popping out of advertising hoardings and monsters coming out of canals, as you can see in the page shown above.

At the end of the book, the poor dog can't even get a good night's sleep because hidden under the flap of the last page is a party of mice climbing up a ladder into his basket.

Evelyn Arizpe and Morag Styles[6] carried out some research to investigate how children respond to the pictures in this and some other classic picture books. When asked what they expected the book to be about by looking at the front cover, the children said things like: 'You think, "What's the dog scared of?" So you, like, turn the page and then look and then just carry on reading and there's some more monsters and you just want to see the rest of it.'[7] The book has the words 'A Spooky Surprise Book' as part of the front cover (see page opposite), but the cartoon-like illustrations and facial expressions hint at something funny. This is why the children's views varied between expecting a funny book or a scary book. This ambiguity is a deliberate device created by the author to foster children's thinking.

The researchers also asked children about the dual plot of the book:

RESEARCHER: Do you think the pictures are telling the same story as the words?

SELMA: Yes, plus a bit more...[the pictures] seem to bring out the story.

In conclusion, the researchers found that children aged four to 11 in their study responded in sophisticated ways to the pictures in the books.

The children,

> *'read colours, borders, body language, framing devices,*
> *covers, endpapers, visual metaphors and visual jokes',*
> *[and] 'most children were keen to discuss the moral,*
> *spiritual and environmental issues [the pictures] raised.*[8]

Pictures are always of interest to children because they are easily accessible and familiar from a very early age. Their exploration of real objects as babies is soon extended to exploring the representation of objects in pictures. TV, films and reading stories add the dimension of pictures linked in a sequence. Once children can decode words, the accompanying pictures also provide alternative storylines and other features of interest.

Which way up?

✪ **As soon as babies are able to use their hands to hold things they should be encouraged to play with books: turn the pages, look at pictures, look at print and talk about all these things.**

Babies need strong books because they will want to explore them by touching, pulling, turning, throwing, tasting, chewing, and so on. Board-books made from heavy card are good because they can withstand this treatment. Not so good in the bath, though, so plastic bath-books are better for that.

Once children's eyes become focused, they'll begin to realize that many things in their environment have to be oriented in a particular way. When children are very young you'll see them pretending to read books, holding them upside down. It's good for your child to explore the physical properties of books, but at some point they will learn that a book has to be held the right way round to access its meaning. Much later they'll learn that English text proceeds from left to right and from top to bottom. Like many things, these seem obvious to fluent readers but they have to be learned by children at some point.

On one occasion, when my two children were reading side-by-side on a big chair, Olly at 1y 10m turned the pages of his *Tellytubbies* book from back to front because he hadn't learned about the orientation of books. Esther, on the other hand, at 3y 10m, understood that you open a book from the right-hand side of the front page and proceed by turning the other pages in the same direction.

Marie Clay[9] included some very useful ideas about orientation as part of her work on reading difficulties. She started her approach in New Zealand, but the success of her ideas soon spread to many other countries. One of her main messages was that early diagnosis of reading problems followed by one-to-one tuition to support children is important. Early diagnosis requires tools to help people judge children's reading development. Clay developed a number of these tools herself and some are still used by researchers to test children's reading.

In relation to orientation of texts, Clay developed the 'Concepts about print test'. This used special booklets that included texts that were deliberately altered. Many of the techniques can be carried out with your child's normal books. I'll explain some of these techniques, not because I think you need to test your child, but because it will raise your awareness of the key concepts your child will learn. The explanation also shows the kinds of questions that you can ask to help your child develop their understanding of orientation of texts. These ideas refer to children learning English, but they can easily be modified for other languages.

Orientation of a book

If you hold a closed book vertically, with the spine towards the child, you can ask them to 'Show me the front of this book.'

Print carries a different message from pictures

Choose a book to read to your child, then say, 'Where are the words?' or 'Where is the writing?' After this you can say, 'Where are the pictures?'

Direction of print

'Let's read this story; you help me; show me where to start reading; where do I begin to read?; show me where to start the text.' Your child should point to the top left of the print in answer to these questions.

'Which way do I go after I've started reading at the beginning?' Your child should show the movement from left to right then stop at the end of the line.

'Where do I go after that?' Your child should return to the left side, ideally at the beginning of the next line.

These questions can also be asked in relation to print which is upside-down to see if the child can recognize inverted print.

Beginning and end

'Show me the beginning of the story.' 'Show me the end of the story.'

Pictures

Show the child a picture that is upside-down. 'Show me the bottom of the picture.' The child can give a verbal explanation or point to the right place or turn the picture round to show you.

Left pages before right pages

'Turn the pages of the book from the beginning towards the end until I ask you to stop.'

Clay's tests then move to a focus on the words, letters and punctuation. One of the important aspects of understanding words is to know what we mean by the word 'word'!

What *is* a word?

Surely it's obvious what a word is? Not as obvious as you might think. Let's start with words in children's spoken language. The vast majority of children learn to speak easily with the support of their parents, family and friends. In the light of this some people have argued that learning to read is just the same as learning to talk. Research tells us that this isn't true. One of the reasons why learning to read is harder than learning to talk is that spoken words are produced and understood in quite different ways from printed words.

Spoken words do not have a gap between them like printed words do. The gaps that we leave when speaking are mainly for pauses to breathe, or for emphasis, or because we lose the thread of what we are saying, or because someone interrupts, and so on. In fact, the biggest difference between speech and print is that speech involves more than one person and is transient, whereas reading and writing are frequently solitary activities where the final draft of text is permanent. In order to read and write, the young child has to learn to segment phrases so that each word in a printed text is separated by a space. Let's just re-run a sentence to experience something similar to the difficulty that a child faces:

Spokenwordsdonothaveagapbetweenthemlikeprintedwordsdo.

It's amazing how much more difficult it is to work out that sentence without the word spaces, even though you read it just a moment ago. The table below shows the main differences between speech and print.

Table showing differences between speech and print

Speech	Print
Requires other speakers to be present at time of speech (unless recorded)	Readers are not present at time of writing
Speakers take turns	Primary writer works alone
Instant and cannot be changed	Can be composed and re-worked
Can be incomplete but make sense because of shared understanding of conversation	Writing usually doesn't make sense if it is not complete
Intonation, pitch and body language used to support meaning	Type effects, such as italics, used to support meaning
Organized in communicative units	Organized in sentences
Separated by pauses in flow of sounds	Separated by punctuation
Words integrated within stream of sounds	Words demarcated by spaces
Consists of phonemes (sounds)	Consists of graphemes (letters)
Accent and dialect are recognisable features of speakers	Accent and dialect do not feature unless used as deliberate devices in fiction or poetry
Tends to be informal	Tends to be formal

It's all in the name

One of the most important words that your child will encounter early on is their name. Here are some games and activities you can use with names and other familiar words.

✪ Whenever you get the chance, encourage your child to read their name, have fun with it, write their name for them and show them the word. When they are ready, show them how to write it and help them with the formation of the letters (see Chapter 4).

✪ Talk about the different sounds in the name.

✪ Write the names of family members and friends and learn those.

✪ When you think that your child is ready, write some labels for everyday objects in the house and stick the words on them: fridge, cupboard, radiator, toy box, Gerry the gerbil's home, and so on.

✪ Talk about words, including asking your child what they think a word is. Ask if they can show you a word.

✪ When reading a book with your child, help them to spot recurring words: characters' names can be a good place to start.

✪ Cutting up texts can be useful. Take a short sentence from a favourite book and rewrite it without any word spaces. Help your child to find the beginnings and ends of the words.

✪ Try cutting a well-known sentence into words then mixing them up. Help your child to put them back into the order of a sentence.

✪ Rewrite the text from each page of a simple book, mount it on card then help your child to match the text in the book with the text on the card.

✪ Play word games like bingo: start by matching pictures and words then move on to words only. Try Pairs/Pelmanism, either bought from a shop or home-made with familiar words such as family names. Later, classic word games will help your child with their spelling and understanding of words: Boggle; Scrabble; Double Quick; crosswords; word searches; Hangman and others.

It's all around you!

Another ideal resource for learning about words is the print in your child's environment. When people talk about learning to read they nearly always have books in mind. But think about the world that the child enters: it's packed with words. From the moment they are born, babies are surrounded by print. The hospital or home where the birth takes place will have greetings cards to welcome the birth. Signs, adverts, newspapers, magazines, books, letters, and so on are all part of your child's print-rich environment. The strong contrast between black print and white paper is something a baby's eyes will focus on very early in life. Later they will recognize print on packaging, for example when you prepare food and drink.

At first, children don't make a distinction between objects and the meaning of print. To see what I mean, imagine a box for a tube of toothpaste. If you removed the text but left the colours of the design, the child would still recognize this as the toothpaste box. Now imagine all the colour and design removed from the box. The brand name is shown, not in its distinctive typeface, but in a plain black one. A very young child, aged one, for example, will not recognize the word 'toothpaste' without its familiar context. Once children are older they learn that print is different from objects, pictures and other designs, and carries a distinct meaning.

Let's look at the sequence of Olly's understanding of print in his environment. When he was 1y 9m he pointed at the words in a book and then said to his mum, 'Wha' tha' say?' (What does that say?) This was the first recorded sign of him thinking about the differences between words and pictures. In the month of his second birthday we read a book with a witch in the story (possibly *Winnie the Witch*). During the reading he pointed at some print and said, 'Wha's this?' I replied, saying 'Writing.' Olly then pointed at the text on the other page and repeated, 'Writing.' This was the first time that we recorded the fact that he actively demonstrated his understanding that there is a difference between print and pictures.

Twenty-two days after his second birthday, Olly was sitting at the table drawing with some felt pens. After a while he said, 'I can't do a D, you do a D.' (He said the correct letter name, 'dee'.) He handed me a pen and I drew two Ds while he made a mark as if he was copying me. Then he spoke to his mum, 'Do a /d/ mummy.' (This time he used the letter sound /d/ to describe the letter.) Olly had already started work on the long journey to understanding how sounds are represented by letters. At this stage he was using two different names for the letter: D and /d/. In time he would become more conscious of the difference between sounds and letter names. Six days after this he was mark-making with wax crayons. At the same time he was saying things like, 'I done a O' or 'Tha's a D': more evidence of his interest in letters and their names. At one point he suddenly shrieked, 'MacDonald's!' When I looked at his paper I saw he'd made a mark like a letter M. He's not the first child for whom the golden arches of the MacDonald's sign have featured in their early understanding of print in the environment (OK, not very *organic* I know!).

At three years old, Olly recognized a text typeface and said, 'That writing should be on *Fireman Sam*,' referring to the TV programme and books that he was keen on at the time. At 3y 6m he was able to reflect on his own reading of environmental print when he closed the door of a CD player: 'I shutted the drawer...I read "open", "shut".' (This awareness is called *metacognitive understanding*.)

✪ **Encouraging your child to consciously think about how they are learning (metacognitive understanding) in addition to directly teaching them is very beneficial.**

Still aged 3y 6m, when out walking in a park, Olly read a sign which said 'NO FISHING'. By this point he was sounding out letters and was able to do this with the capital letters in the sign.

A month later he was playing the game Ludo with his sister. He pointed to the word 'HOME' which was written on the board, covered the 'E' with his hand, read the word and said, 'It doesn't need the E.' Here was a very early example of him realising that trying to sound out every letter in a word doesn't always work. This built the foundation of his knowledge of the 'magic E', or 'modifying E', rule. On another occasion, during a journey in the car, he saw a Peugeot car dealership and said, 'They only sell Peugeots in there.'

The final example of Olly learning to read environmental print once again shows his metacognitive understanding. He was looking at a pack of toilet rolls:

OLLY: That says Tesco.
DAD: How do you know?
OLLY: Because I read the word.

Quite so! Notice the way that my question, 'How do you know?' deliberately encouraged Olly to reflect on his own understanding.

It's important to remember that although some of the most important lessons are learned by sharing books, the world of environmental print also offers exciting opportunities for learning. You need to engage with your child's natural interest in all print to help them to learn more.

✪ **Use every opportunity with print and other text in the environment to talk about words and reading.**

Within reach of sticky fingers

Once you've started to collect books for your child, it's important that they are kept in a way that will help your child's learning.

✪ **Store books somewhere that's easy for your child to reach so that at any time they can go and choose a book.**

Normally, the room that you spend most time in, such as a living/sitting room, is a good main place for keeping books. A low shelf or other kind of low-level storage is essential. Involve your child in tidying this from time to time, as not only does this train them in the good habit of tidying up, but it reminds them of all the books that are on the shelf, too. Your child will also need a good selection of books in the bedroom which they can reach easily on their own. As they get older, this may well become their main collection to choose from as reading material before they go to sleep and at other times.

Big sister can help!

In this chapter I've talked a lot about children's natural capacity to learn and what you can do to help them. I want to finish by showing that it's not only your influence that's beneficial. What about the role of older brothers and sisters? A large part of Olly's early success as a reader was due to the good influence of his sister.

A video clip taken when Olly was only 1y 10m and Esther was

3y 10m dramatically shows this. At the time, we had a really wide, old armchair which had taken a bit of a battering from cats' claw marks. Both children were sitting side-by-side, separately reading books of their choice. Esther was reading *Willy the Wizard*, by Anthony Browne, and Olly was reading *Tellytubies and the Flying Toast*. You can see the front covers of the books below. Esther was singing, 'Willy the Wizard' over and over again as she turned the pages of her book. Olly was turning the pages of his book starting with the ones at the end and moving towards the pages at the beginning.

ESTHER: **Willy the Wizard** [*repeated singing*].

OLLY: **Finished** [*he opens the book again at the beginning*]. **The end.**

ESTHER: **The end /um/** [*throws her book onto the floor*].

OLLY: **Read the Teletubbies** [*request*].

ESTHER: **Teletubbies and flying** [*singsong voice*] **flying, flying, flying, flying, flying, flying, flying, flying, flying, flying.**

OLLY: **Read it, then.**

ESTHER: **Flying, flying, flying.**

OLLY: **Read it, then.**

ESTHER: **Toast, flying toast, toast, flying toast /la/ Olly I need to bend it a bit** [*folds front cover behind the book*]. **Right, who's that?**

OLLY: **Noo Noo.**

ESTHER: **Yep! Noo Noo** [*turns to next page*].

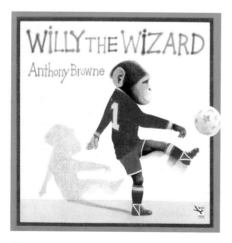

Willie the Wizard, by Anthony Browne, Red Fox

Tellytubbies and the Flying Toast, BBC Children's Books

ESTHER: **Who's that Ol?**

OLLY: **Noo Noo.**

ESTHER: **Who's that?**

OLLY: **Noo Noo.**

ESTHER: **Who' that?!** [*getting slightly exasperated*].

OLLY: **Noo Noo.**

ESTHER: **No, it's not Noo Noo, who is that?**

OLLY: **Don't know!**

ESTHER: **It's a Teletubby and it's La La, OK?**

OLLY: **La La.**

ESTHER: **Tinky Winky...Delicious** [*Olly seems to imitate the word 'delicious'. Esther turns the page*]. **Now, let's see what happens now... noises, slurp slurpy slurp slurpy, sloop sloop slurpy slurp slurpy. Uh-oh!** [*meaning oh dear; sung like a held musical note*]. **[What's] gonna happen Ol?** [*turns page*] **Oh dear me me me, all the Tubby's toast is falling out isn't it? Ooh, that's falling out. Shall we see what happens now? Oh look at all those Ol** [*holds picture of toast up to Olly's face for him to lick*].

OLLY: **Yeah.**

ESTHER: **Don't eat it...eat at all the toast** [*both children take it in turns to pretend to eat the toast in the picture. Esther then realizes that it's fun to really lick the picture. They both take it in turns to do this, laughing more and more*].

Esther was full of confidence that she could read the book to Olly even though she could not decode the words. She clearly explained to him certain things that had to be done, like bending the cover of the book back. She used a range of questions, for example to see if he knew who some of the characters were and to ask him what he thought was going to happen next in the story. She drew his attention to things in the pictures, such as the Tubby Toast falling out of the machine. She was careful to stop him doing things that he shouldn't, such as eating the toast, until her sense of fun got the better of her and they both played a game of actually licking the picture of the toast on the page. Esther showed sophisticated teaching strategies which helped Olly's learning.

Guidelines for what to expect

By the age of four you should expect your child to be showing the reading behaviour listed in the table on the page opposite. This will be your expectation, because high expectations have a positive effect, but don't worry unduly if your child is not showing all these signs of development. These are general characteristics for many children but some children develop more slowly at first. Other children will have gone beyond this and may be showing some, or all, of the reading behaviour explained in the next chapter. If so, it's a very good thing and should be praised. The table also summarizes the kinds of things that you should be doing with your child to encourage their development at this stage. There are similar 'what to expect' sections at the end of each chapter in this book.

Expectations for a child's reading at four years old

What you can expect	What you can do to help
Understands distinction between print and pictures.	Talk about pictures and talk about print. Encourage your child to point to print or point to pictures.
Can recognize and understand some words and signs in the environment.	Encourage your child to read food packets and to play 'shop'. Read signs, logos and labels with them. Comment on text that appears on TV. Talk about greetings cards.
Understands that text has specific meaning.	Read stories and other books with your child. When reading a text that's at the child's level, read all the words as written. Talk about what particular words and sentences mean.
Plays at reading.	Make sure that your child has easy access to a really good range of books. Encourage their playing with the books and their pretend reading. Encourage them to pretend to read to others or even to cuddly toys.
Uses words and phrases from written language when retelling stories.	Respond to your child's request to hear favourite stories. Encourage your child to predict what is coming next in a story. Suggest that they join in with repetitive phrases. Celebrate when they remember phrases from favourite stories.
Needs other people to help with reading aloud.	Read aloud daily with your child. Encourage discussion and always look to develop your child's independence to read words.
Will choose favourite picture books to be read aloud.	Read daily. Provide easy access to books. Read your child's favourites but remember you can have some choice as well!
Uses picture cues and memory of texts.	Once your child is familiar with a book, encourage them to tell the story by looking at the pictures.
Understands orientation of print and books.	Talk about the front and back covers of books, where the print is, where the print starts on a page. Comment on books that play with these conventions.
Salient visual cues used to remember some familiar words like own name.	Give frequent opportunities to read, write and play games with words such as names.

age four
to seven

Old favourites and new challenges

This is one of the most exciting stages of them all because you see your child move from reading words and short phrases to reading simple sentences and whole books fluently. As I take you through this chapter, we'll delve into the world of phonemes (sounds) and letters. But I want to underline the fact that knowledge about letters and phonemes is only one important part of learning to read. There's an ever-present risk that the purpose of reading, which is for pleasure and learning, can be lost in an unduly narrow focus on skills.

✪ **One of the key things to get right when helping your child is the balance between developing skills and reading for real. That said, from the age of five onwards the knowledge of phonemes and letters temporarily becomes really important.**

Whole texts come first, so I begin this section just like the other reading sections, with some examples of wonderful books and an explanation of why they help your child's reading. I don't want to imply that the books I discussed in the previous section will now be completely abandoned. On the contrary, children need to re-read texts that are favourites throughout their life. There's something very comforting about this. I remember the times when I've had to sort through the kids' bookshelves to make space for new books. As I tried my hardest to transfer some of the books to the loft, the kids would be eagerly leafing through the box and pulling out the books they'd forgotten they had, and back on the shelves some of them would go. Involving children in the reorganization of books from time to time can be a good way to remind them of what's available.

✪ **For reasons of space you'll need to remove books from children's shelves occasionally, but always leave some 'old friends'. They are a good reminder to your child of how far they have travelled along the learning-to-read journey.**

Wonderful books – age four to seven

The book I've chosen to illustrate the best for children from age four to seven is *So Much*, written by Trish Cooke and illustrated by Helen

Oxenbury.[1] Prizes are only one way of judging books but, on this occasion, the awards of the Smarties Book Prize, the Kurt Maschler Award and the She/W. H. Smith awards were an excellent guide. Anthony Browne, another of my favourite picture-book authors, is quoted on the back cover:

It is always a delight to see an established artist taking risks, breaking new ground and succeeding brilliantly.

The story begins like this:

They weren't doing anything
Mum and the baby
nothing really...
Then,
DING DONG!
"Oooooooh!"
Mum looked at the door,
the baby looked at Mum.
It was...

The scene is set, and it's a familiar one to mothers and children. In the first picture the baby is standing on the settee looking through the window and mum is kneeling next to the baby. The doorbell rings. The use of capital letters for the sound of the bell shows the way it cuts through the mother's and child's daydreaming. The baby calls out 'Oooooooh!', with seven Os and an exclamation mark. This adds more sound, one of the many brilliant features of the book. Then the text encourages children to predict who has rung the doorbell by leaving a mini cliff-hanger until you turn the page. This helps to develop an important reading strategy and recognizes children's enthusiasm for guessing and problem solving: Who do you think is at the door?

Auntie,
Auntie Bibba.
Auntie Bibba came inside with her
arms out wide, wide, wide
and one big smile.

"Oooooooh!" she said.
"I want to squeeze him,
I want to squeeze the baby,
I want to squeeze him
SO MUCH!"

The structure of the story has now been set. Repetition is a vital part of all good picture books, but it has to be carefully handled so as not to slip into being boring. As each new character arrives at the house, they first want to do something different with the baby, such as squeeze him (Auntie Bibba), kiss him (Uncle Didi), eat him (Nanny and Gran-Gran), fight him (Cousin Kay Kay and Big Cousin Ross):

And they wrestle
and they wrestle.
He push the baby first,
the baby hit him back.
He gave the baby pinch,
the baby gave him slap.
And then they laugh
and laugh and laugh.
"Huh huh huh!"

The illustrations show sensitive and positive images, with a sense of fun, of a British Afro-Caribbean extended family. The language of the book uses superbly some of the rhythms and repetitions of African English, which links it with other writers such as the Guyanese poet John Agard. The core feature of the book is a universally understood idea, a child-and-adult game like 'How big's baby?' or 'How much do we love you?'

As the book reaches its climax a big group of people are playing and talking, but still the reader wants to know why they are there.

"SURPRISE!"
everybody said,
and Mum said,
"HAPPY BIRTHDAY, DADDY!"
and everybody joined in.

After the double page with no text, showing everyone dancing, laughing, playing, eating ice-creams and drinking fizzy drinks (a layout feature that Maurice Sendak uses in the classic picture book *Where The Wild Things Are*), everybody has to go home and baby has to go to sleep in his cot. But he's too excited, so:

> *The baby played*
> *bounce-bounce with Ted,*
> *played bounce-bounce in his cot,*
> *and he remembered*
> *everybody saying*
> *how they wanted*
> *to SQUEEZE*
> *and KISS*
> *and EAT*
> *and FIGHT him...*

On the final page, there's a picture of the baby asleep next to his teddy, and mum and dad tucking him in:

> *because they loved him*
> *SO MUCH!*

And now, to summarize the key features of *So Much*:

✪ The setting is familiar but there is plenty to arouse curiosity in your child.

✪ The use of language is wonderful, ranging from sublime rhythms and repetitions to the clever use of punctuation and layout.

✪ The pictures are realistic and artistically accomplished.

✪ Prediction is encouraged.

✪ There is a satisfying repetition which helps your child's memory of the story. This is enhanced by the introduction of new characters and the different ways that they play with the baby.

The table on the following page shows some more books that I recommend when your child is this age. You'll see that I include two recommendations that are aimed specifically at either a boy or a girl. From this stage onwards, preferences relating to your child's gender often become stronger.

As long as they read!

The table on the right shows some more types of books that your child will enjoy at this age. It doesn't matter what children read (within what you feel is morally appropriate), as long as they do read something. For me, this is a guiding principle about learning to read and becoming a life-long enthusiastic reader. Schools will expose children to a variety of texts selected for teaching, in line with the English curriculum, so home should be a place where children get real choices over what they read (frankly, they should also get plenty of choice at school as well). When children exercise their choices, one of the outcomes is that boys and girls frequently have different tastes. The marketing of books for children, particularly at about the age of seven, shows this markedly, as a quick browse of your local bookshop shelves will show. For example, you may notice the *occasional* pink book cover for girls!

Books for children aged four to seven

Type of book	Example
A classic picture book	*Where the Wild Things Are*, by Maurice Sendak
Picture book with cartoon features	*Traction Man is Here*, by Mini Grey
A poetry book	*Poems for the Very Young*, selected by Michael Rosen, illustrated by Bob Graham
Books designed explicitly to help reading	*Green Eggs and Ham*, by Dr Seuss
Innovative book technology	*The Jolly Postman or Other People's Letters*, by Janet and Allan Ahlberg
An information book	*Mummy Laid an Egg!*, by Babette Cole
An information book with innovative technology	*Let's look inside: the Body*, a First Discovery/Torchlight book. Illustrated by Pierre-Marie Valat
A5 format with girl as main character	*It's not fair!*, by Bel Mooney
A5 format with boy as main character	*Horrid Henry's Stinkbomb*, by Francesca Simon

Why is it good?	Any limitations?	By same author
Childhood experience of being naughty. The structure of the book, reflected by layout, use of language and distinctive artwork is superb. Use of language is unique.	None	*Brundibar*
Uses a child's imaginative play with an action figure as basis for language in the book. The book is really funny and the humour will appeal to children and adults.	Episodic rather than strong narrative which will appeal to some more than others.	*The Adventures of the Dish and the Spoon*
After nursery rhymes it is difficult to find good poems for young children. This anthology does it very well. The illustrator Bob Graham has authored his own good picture books, such as *Baby Brains*.	None	Many excellent books
The Dr Seuss books achieve the distinction of focusing on rhyme, repetition and simple words without being dull. Zany humour.	Word play comes before narrative.	Many excellent books
A stunning early example of book technology with inserts, such as letters, an invitation, a fairytale book, and a birthday card. Fairytale characters permeate the story, told in rhyming couplets. A gem.	None	Many excellent books
This is really a storybook, but it shows how fiction and non-fiction share important features. The children give naïve mum and dad some sex education. So cleverly written that most people would be happy to share it with young children despite the topic.	Will challenge some parents' views about what is appropriate for children.	Many excellent books
Features a card 'torch' which really seems to illuminate the pages when you insert it underneath the acetates that are in the book.	Torch tends to get lost easily.	*Paintings* (First Discovery/Art Series)
Familiar family scenes for parents and children written in a lively and engaging way.	A rather small world for the characters.	*Who Loves Mr Tubs?* (Blue Bananas Series)
Great fun, with a humour that manages to appeal to both adults and children.	None	*Horrid Henry's Evil Enemies*

As far as my children are concerned, their different interests began at a young age. Olly pursued his relentlessly. I remember, at about one year old he seemed to be obsessed with holes. Wherever he found them he had to explore them. This was replaced by an interest in toy cars: driving them along the floor, lining them up in a traffic jam, organising them in a car park, and many other kinds of play with them. This interest in toy cars spread to books. Here's an example from when he was 2y 5m. He was at the breakfast table one morning, flicking through the pages of an *I Spy Book of Cars*. The text in these books is really quite demanding and probably suitable for children of about eight. Despite this, he really enjoyed flicking through the pages and looking at the pictures of all the different cars.

OLLY: That's like Grandma's car...Grandma and granddad's car...my car.
DAD: Is it?
OLLY: Yeah!
DAD: What colour is it?
OLLY: Blue.
DAD: Oh right.
OLLY: That's a funny car
DAD: Is it?
OLLY: Yeah!

By comparison, Esther has always loved fiction and has rarely shown interest in factual books, although it should be remembered that schoolwork increasingly emphasizes non-fiction texts as children move through the system.

Esther and Olly's preferences mirror, to a certain extent, our interests. Their mum is an avid fiction reader, while I tend to be more eclectic, mixing reading fiction with non-fiction related to my writing and work, and other non-fiction out of general curiosity. This raises the important point that you provide a role-model as a reader for your child.

✪ **As the role-model of a reader for your child, let them see you reading, talk to them about what you enjoy reading and discuss whatever they are reading. Overall, you should encourage your child to develop personal interests in particular authors and types of books. You'll still get many opportunities to recommend books to them that you hope they will read.**

Reading schemes v. 'real' books

There has been much debate about the merits of reading scheme books (or *basal* readers as they say in the USA) versus 'real' books, like the wonderful ones I have recommended in this book. Many schools use a mixture of reading scheme books and real books. The advantage of real books is that they feature the talents of authors whose goal is to create exciting texts that will interest children and make them think. On the other hand, reading scheme books are written specially to help with teaching reading. They have a controlled vocabulary that ensures that children are exposed repeatedly to high-frequency words which they should begin to remember. Unfortunately, this can result in a poor quality of text overall, despite the advantages of the controlled vocabulary. Here's an example of the text from one of the books in the GINN 360 reading scheme[2] that has been popular for many years.

Help!
Where is Dad?
Dad, can you help?
I can help.

Many people have commented on the disjointed flow that such books have because of their controlled vocabulary. You may also have noticed that there are no speech marks: presumably it's felt that young children will be confused by such things. Although you can still find some rather shocking and amusing examples of old-fashioned reading scheme texts, in recent years publishers have brought out newer reading schemes that address such problems. But they will still always be different from real books.

You'll probably find that reading scheme books are the ones that get sent home by the school for you to help with your child's reading (there's an example of Esther reading a scheme book that had been sent home in the section 'When will the magical moment come?', on page 63). Sometimes parents are sent two books, one from a scheme and a real book. Other schools and settings just send a real book. If reading scheme books are used at all, they are probably best used with children aged between five and six.

✪ **Children are motivated most by reading real, exciting books. As soon as they can decode simple reading scheme books well, these should be abandoned in favour of real books, at home and at school.**

Unfortunately, there are examples of schools where children are shackled to a reading scheme until the junior years, by which time any motivation to read for pleasure has been squashed by the limited nature of the reading scheme texts. The wealth of children's books available in shops means that there should never be a shortage of relevant texts for children in schools. I would not advise you to buy reading scheme texts for your child. Use real books to help them learn to read in the ways suggested in this book.

Is it the right level?

One of the things that might concern you is how to choose books with text that's at the appropriate level for your child to read. The best way to do this is to take your child with you to the library or bookshop and allow a bit of time to browse (and perhaps include a coffee and hot chocolate at some point!). Here are some things you can do:

✪ While browsing through books, show your child how to look at the cover to see if it interests them.
✪ See if they can read some of the book. They should be able to read at least 75 per cent of the words.
✪ Explain that it's often a good idea to test-read the first page and/ or flick through the whole book to see if it catches their imagination.

It's important to remember that a few books that are *beyond* your child's reading level are still relevant. Most good books for young children have pictures which are easily accessible, even if the text is too difficult.

Besides, it's rare that all the words in a text are too hard. Fiction books tend to need the closest match between the book and your child's reading level. Non-fiction, on the other hand, can be accessed in different ways. It includes more headings, captions and so on, which children can benefit from even if some of the other text is too difficult.

✪ **Be aware that attempting a few books that are beyond your child's reading level may act as an incentive to learn to read better.**
✪ **To help further, you can read difficult books aloud to your child so that they start to pick up the language, which eventually they will be able to read independently.**

There are more scientific ways to judge readability. For example, standardized reading tests sometimes include comprehension tests which feature sequences of paragraphs, graded on the basis of analysis of the words they contain, and arranged in levels of difficulty. More subjective methods, which fit better with the kinds of advice that I have just given, are also available. For example, Cliff Moon's[3] popular readability levels, based on his approach to individualized reading, have been successful. Moon lists books according to 12 stages. His booklet shows the stages alongside alphabetic lists of the publishers of reading schemes and real books, with examples of books that fit within the level. To give you an idea, the *Kipper Story Collection*, featuring Kipper the puppy, is one of the examples given for Moon's Stage 8 under the 'Hodder paperbacks' entry. This stage is equivalent to the National Curriculum Level 2 (the average level for seven-year-olds).

Official readability measures give a reasonable guide to a book's level, but if you follow my advice in the first paragraph of this section, *you* will be a far better guide to the books that are suitable because you will have day-to-day knowledge about your child's reading level and interests. Technical readability levels are not the most important concern for parents. In some ways, the issue is similar to standardized reading test scores which can be converted to reading ages. Although reading tests give a reasonable guide to a child's reading at any particular point in time, what they cannot do is predict how a child's reading will progress in future. They are also much less use as children get older. What is your reading age, or mine, or any other adult's for that matter?

Top Ten things to think about for children's books

Age: four to seven

1 Is the subject of the book one that will interest your child?

2 In what ways does the book link with your child's world and offer new perspectives?

3 Is the narrative strong?

4 Will the book engage your child's curiosity?

5 Is the balance between pictures and the amount of text right for your child?

6 Is the level of the text appropriate for your child?

7 What kind of knowledge might your child acquire by reading the book?

8 Is the structure of the book effective and satisfying?

9 Is the use of language good?

10 Will the book support your child's learning?

When will the magical moment come?

One of the most magical moments in your child's development is when they learn to read the words in a sentence. I've said that this is a 'moment', but it's difficult to pinpoint an exact moment when your child is 'really' reading like this. Can you remember when you learned to read? It's difficult isn't it? I have an image of when I learned to read. I was staying with an aunt who regularly looked after me and my brother. Just before I went to sleep, I was reading a book called *Daddy, Read me a Bedtime Story* – I think that was the title, anyway. The right-hand pages of the book had quite long sections of text; the pictures were on the left-hand pages. Previously, I would have flicked through the book simply remembering the stories that had been read to me. But on this particular night I remember thinking, I can read those words! They matched the memory of the story that I had in my head. It was almost like mist clearing from a blurred image.

The stage I'm talking about is when your child develops the ability to read words as part of a sentence. In order to show you how this vital stage might be reached, let's look at how Esther developed.

When Esther was 2y 1m the following conversation took place:

ESTHER: What's it say, daddy?

DAD: It says, 'Mamas & Papas' [*printed on her high chair*].

ESTHER: Mama in the arbour [*reference to picture book*].

This exchange showed that Esther understood that print has a specific meaning, and also that she knew there was a difference between words and pictures. She also related the word 'mama' to a phrase that she had heard in the book *Outside Over There*, by Maurice Sendak – a wonderful, but slightly unnerving story. At 2y 6m she recognized her name amongst a list of four names. At 3y 6m I was reading a simple text by Brian Wildesmith (1982) called *Cat on the Mat*, which Esther knew from memory. For the first time she waited until my finger was pointing at the words before she said them. At 3y 8m Esther chose the book *So Much* to be read to her. I asked her what it was called. Before this point, she would have said that she didn't know. On this occasion, she sounded out the /s/ for 'So' then blended /m/ and /uch/. This was the first evidence that we collected of her segmenting and blending sounds rather than using memory and picture clues. At 3y 10m Esther read *Cat on the Mat* to me word-perfectly. I then played a game of spotting words in the book with her by saying, 'Which word says…?' I also tried to trick her by pretending that a word had a different meaning, but she spotted this, so it was clear that she was reading words in this very well-known text.

The first video evidence showing Esther's ability to decode the words of an unknown text came at 4y 6m. It's important to point out that reading unknown text is different from reading familiar story texts and is a very significant moment in reading development. We were on the settee looking at the book together – it was a reading scheme that had been sent home by her school (the picture below shows the text).

Stop it.
It is not here.
It is not in my home.

A page from a Ginn Reading Scheme book

ESTHER: I, /k/ /a/ /n/, can not find it.

DAD: Hmm, good guess. That's not 'find' is it?

ESTHER: /h/, /h/ Help, me, look, where is it.

DAD: No [*I was indicating that 'where is it' was not in the text*], 'Stop' [*offering the word in text*].

ESTHER: Stop it, it is not here.

DAD: Well done.

ESTHER: It is not /no/ [*Esther departs from the text here. The printed word is 'in'. She sees the second letter N and guesses the rest of the word as 'no'*] it not.

DAD: in [*I refocus her attention on the word in the text*].

ESTHER: in.

In one sense, Esther's reading seemed to have gone backwards. She was reading less fluently than when she used to read stories using memory. Working out the words was slow and laborious. This is a quite normal temporary phenomenon. Once your child starts to use phonological knowledge (knowing the links between sounds and letters) to read words, they will be slow at first until the words start to become part of their *sight-word memory*, which means they become part of a rapidly increasing number of words that are automatically recognized because they are stored in long-term memory. The other thing to point out is that this reading scheme text was not very interesting and was most unlike the real books that Esther was used to.

This is the stage when children really need to get to grips with phonemes (sounds) and the way that letters in words represent them. Esther and Olly's sequence of development of phonological knowledge started with an interest in the overall meaning of signs and other print in the environment. This was followed by a focus on whole words and word chunks in other contexts. Finally, they were helped to segment phonemes in words and to blend phonemes together to read words, but always in the context of reading real books. Overall, this was a progression from larger units of language to smaller ones.

One of the things that helps with learning to decode is pointing at the words. When your child points at the words you can tell if they have developed one-to-one correspondence.

✪ It can be helpful for you to point to the words as your child reads them, with your finger or a pencil. It draws their attention to the word they are focusing on and helps to stop them losing their place.

✪ At this stage you'll notice that your child, who could tell you stories from memory quite fluently, starts to read very slowly, a bit like a robot. It's agony at times, but resist the temptation always to give them the word too quickly.

✪ If your child is struggling with a difficult word, a good strategy can be to ask if they want you to tell them the word.

✪ Often, if children are given enough time, they do manage to work out words on their own. If they really don't know a word you can simply tell them.

In answer to the question at the start of this section, I think that if you put into practice my advice in this book your child should be able to decode simple unknown and less-well-known texts between the ages of four and five, and this would represent an early start. I would expect many children to reach this magic moment between the ages of five and six. Children who don't decode by the age of seven are a cause for concern, but should not induce high levels of anxiety. It simply means that they are likely to need more support in school, based on a full understanding of the many factors that can be responsible for children not learning to read early.

English – the hardest language

One of the main challenges for children learning to read in English is that it is the hardest language of them all to learn. The reason that some languages are easier to learn than others is to do with their complexity. As Usha Goswami[4] has shown, there are two key factors in this.

The first is the way that consonants and vowels are linked together. Some languages, such as Italian, Spanish and Chinese, are based on a simple consonant-vowel syllable structure (like *casa* which means house in Italian, or *hola* which means hello in Spanish). This makes them less complex than English. English has very few consonant-vowel syllables. Words such as 'baby' and 'cocoa' are examples that do exist (see the grid at the top of the page opposite). The most frequent syllable type in English is consonant-vowel-consonant, as in words like 'dog' and 'cat'.

Some words in English with consonant-vowel syllables

Word	Syllable	Consonant	Vowel(s)	Syllable	Consonant	Vowel(s)
baby	ba	b	a	by	b	y
cocoa	co	c	o	coa	c	oa

The second key factor is the consistency of how the written symbols represent sounds. In some languages, such as English and Dutch, one letter or one cluster of letters can have many different pronunciations. In other languages, such as Greek, Italian and Spanish, the letters and clusters are always pronounced in the same way no matter what word they appear in, which is obviously simpler to learn.

Vowels in English are particularly tricky. Let me illustrate. How would you say this word: 'read'? You might well say it sounds like this: /r/ /ee/ /d/. And if the word is put into a context, like this: 'Today I am going to read a book', you'd be right. But what if the context was: 'Yesterday I read a book'? The two letters in the middle of the word (ea) change their sound from /ee/ to /e/ because the context of the sentence has changed. This reaches the height of absurdity in the title of the university department once called 'The Centre for Reading in Reading', which was in the city of Reading! A large study of 14 European languages (see the table below) clearly showed the dramatic differences in the ease of reading real words and made-up words in different languages, with English right at the bottom of the list.

Data (% correct) from the large-scale study of reading skills at the end of Grade 1 in 14 European languages[5]

Language	Familiar real words	Pseudo words
Greek	98	92
Finnish	98	95
German	98	94
Austrian German	97	92
Italian	95	89
Spanish	95	89
Swedish	95	88
Dutch	95	82
Icelandic	94	86
Norwegian	92	91
French	79	85
Portuguese	73	77
Danish	71	54
Scottish English	34	29

Research has shown that children need to learn about the links between phonemes and letters if they are to progress from early reading behaviour to the decoding of words. This learning needs to take place in the context of reading real texts for real purposes.

✪ **Sharing books with your child and discussing print in the environment are ideal contexts to talk about phonemes (sounds) and letters.**

For children aged four to seven, these discussions will be much more frequent than for younger or older children. One reason for this is that your child's natural development tends to arrive at a point when they are curious about sounds and symbols. It's also because formal education focuses on phonics, which is the teaching of phonemes to help with reading, in the years from five onwards.

Sounds and letters

I've already explained that English is one of the most complex languages to decipher. Fortunately, nearly all children can rise to the challenge with relative ease if they get the right support. This would not be possible if they literally had to memorize every single sound-symbol relationship. There are just too many to consciously memorize. This children's joke reveals the complexity:

CHILD 1: **Will you remember me tomorrow?**
CHILD 2: **Yes.**
CHILD 1: **Will you remember me in a week?**
CHILD 2: **Yes.**
CHILD 1: **Will you remember me in a month?**
CHILD 2: **Yes.**
CHILD 1: **Will you remember me in a year?**
CHILD 2: **Yes.**
CHILD 1: **Knock, knock!**
CHILD 2: **Who's there?**
CHILD 1: **You've forgotten me already!**

I recall working with one of the five-year-old children in my class who was writing this joke as part of her joke book. She asked me how to spell the word 'remember'. I suggested that she try and sound it out by using her phonological knowledge. As I was saying this, I realized that the word 'remember' has the letter E three times, and each time it represents a different phoneme: /r/ /ee/ /m/ /e/ m/ /b/ /uh/. This means that if you suggest to children that the letter E makes the /e/ sound, you are only giving them one small part of the facts. Fortunately, as I've said, children don't need to learn every single sound-symbol relationship because, with just enough information, they start to self-teach. However, it's useful if *you* are aware of the 44 phonemes because this will guide your interaction with your child and enable you to give accurate information at the right time.

The English language has 26 letters which are used to represent 44 phonemes or sounds. All the words in the English language are *spoken* using combinations of the 44 phonemes. All the words in the English language are *written* using combinations of the 26 letters. The table on the next page shows you all 44 phonemes. It's organized into consonant phonemes and vowel phonemes.

Some strange things about letters

One thing that might come as a surprise is the way that different groups of letters represent the same sound. For example, if you look at the vowel phoneme /ie/ which is the long I sound, you can see that the examples of words given are 'tr**ie**d, l**igh**t, m**y**, sh**i**ne, m**i**nd'. The idea that the letters 'igh' represent the /ie/ sound seems distinctly odd doesn't it? The old-fashioned way would be to say that these letters sound as /i/ /g/ /h/. But if you said this, it would mean that you'd pronounce the word 'light' as 'liguhut' which, of course, would be ridiculous (although this can be one useful strategy to remember spellings, see Chapter 6)! So, it's quite accurate to say that the /ie/ sound in the spoken word can be represented in the written word by the letters 'ie' or 'igh' or 'y' or 'ine' (where the 'magic e' means that 'i' is here pronounced /ie/).

A very basic, but important, aspect of letters can be explained by thinking about the special kinds of objects that they are. Imagine that you are holding a chair. Next, you turn it upside-down. What is it now? Yes, it's still a chair, but it's an upside-down chair. Now imagine that you have a large-sized, lower-case letter in your hand, let's say the letter 'p'. If you turn it upside-down it changes from a letter 'p' to a letter 'b', well from the child's point of view, anyway. You've got to mind your lower-case 'p's and 'q's as well! And what about the troublesome letter I? Sometimes it's not even a letter at all, it's a word: 'I went to the shops' (and to cap it all, it could be confused with the word 'eye', when spoken). At other times, it can so easily become a number 1 – hang on a minute, was that a letter I? (This looked identical on my laptop until I increased the zoom and then I could just about see that the number was wider than the letter.) In other words, objects do not change just because you turn them round, but letters and numbers can appear to. This aspect of the nature of print has to be understood by children, along with many other things, as they progress towards reading and writing.

Phonemes and representative words

Consonant phonemes

Consonant phonemes	International Phonetic Alphabet	Representative words
/b/	b	baby
/d/	d	dog
/f/	f	field, photo
/g/	g	game
/h/	h	hat
/j/	dʒ	judge, giant, barge
/k/	k	cook, quick, mix, Chris
/l/	l	lamb
/m/	m	monkey, comb
/n/	n	nut, knife, gnat
/ng/	ŋ	ring, sink
/p/	p	paper
/r/	r	rabbit, wrong
/s/	s	sun, mouse, city, science
/t/	t	tap
/v/	v	van
/w/	w	was
/y/	j	yes
/z/	z	zebra, please, is
/th/	ð	then
/th/	θ	thin
/ch/	tʃ	chip, watch
/sh/	ʃ	ship, mission, chef
/zh/	ʒ	treasure

UPPER and lower case

Next are the difficulties with lower and upper case. Your child will learn
that letters have two different forms. Understanding when to use the
different forms takes you into the area of grammar. Substantive nouns,
such as people's names, have a capital letter. Some words in titles have
capital letters. The first letter of a sentence has a capital letter, but
to understand this you have to understand how to define a sentence
(see Chapter 5). Words like OK are written with capitals. Then, to
complicate everything further, they will see lots of examples of print
in the environment, on computers and on mobile phones where capital
letters are missing altogether. Although this is complicated, the fact that
you understand these things means that you'll be able to help your child
understand why letters work in the way that they do.

Vowel phonemes

Vowel phonemes	International Phonetic Alphabet	Representative words
/a/	æ	cat
/e/	ɛ	peg, bread
/i/	ɪ	pig, wanted
/o/	ɒ	log, want
/u/	ʌ	plug, love
/ae/	eɪ	pain, day, gate, station
/ee/	iː	sweet, heat, thief, these
/ie/	aɪ	tried, light, my, shine, mind
/oe/	əʊ	road, blow, bone, cold
/ue/	uː	moon, blue, grew, tune
/oo/	ʊ	look, would, put
/ar/	ɑː	cart, fast (regional)
/ur/	ɜː	burn, first, term, heard, work
/au/	ɔː	torn, door, warn, haul, law, call
/er/	ə	wooden, circus, sister
/ow/	aʊ	down, shout
/oi/	ɔɪ	coin, boy
/air/	ɛə	stairs, bear, hare
/ear/	ɪə	fear, beer, here
/ure/	ʊə	pure, tourist

Naming names

The best way to talk about letters is to refer to their names. Just as you wouldn't call a chair a pig, so it doesn't make sense to call the letter A the /a/ sound all the time, because the /a/ sound is not the letter's name. Try to get into the habit of using the proper letter names when you are referring to letters.

If you think that this is all too complicated for young children, see how these three-year-olds in a nursery discussed the subject:

DOMINIC: **Oh that's good, a parcel for Ben, I like that. I'll take a picture of it like that.**

MARK: **I want to hold it like that.**

DOMINIC: **Do you? That makes the writing upside down, is that all right? OK. You want to hold it. Well, tip it back a bit so that I can get the writing. Look at the camera, you can see it...That looks like a letter M.**

MICHAEL: **No it's a /m/.**

DOMINIC: **It's a /m/ is it?**

MICHAEL: **/m/ for mummy. It's for my mummy.**

NEIL: **No, it's M for mummy.**

DOMINIC: **That's right, M is the name of the letter isn't it, and /m/ is the sound.**

NEIL: **No, M!**

DOMINIC: **M's the name, yes. They're both right. Is that mummy?**

NEIL: **Yes.**

And here's an extract that I'll discuss in more detail in the writing part of the book. Olly, aged 5y 4m, was doing some writing. Once again, you see the way that children deal with the difference between letters' names and their associated phonemes. In this example, Olly is faced with the classic difficulty that the letter C can represent either a soft sound /s/ or a hard sound /k/.

OLLY: **[How do you] spell ice-cream?**

DAD: **I, C, E.**

OLLY: **I,...C.**

DAD: **That's right.**

OLLY: **E, E, /k/. [Is] that /k/?**

DAD: C, yeah.

OLLY: /k/ /r/ /reem/. What's after /r/? Dad, what's after /r/?

DAD: What's after what?

OLLY: What's af...

DAD: Um, C, R, E, A, M.

OLLY: E,..A,...ice-cream...Pink ice-cream out.

Children's knowledge of the names of the letters of the alphabet when they start reception class has been shown to be a very good indicator of later success in reading and writing. Here are some things you can do which help with learning the alphabet.

✪ Sing alphabet songs.

✪ Play I-spy, sometimes with sounds and sometimes with letter names:

ADULT: I spy with my little eye something beginning with the sound /k/.

CHILD: Cat!

ADULT: I spy with my little eye something beginning with the letter D.

CHILD: Dog!

✪ Put up an alphabet frieze which shows all the letters of the alphabet with a corresponding picture so that you can talk to your child about the names of the letters.

✪ Put magnetic letters on the fridge. The plastic ones are fine, but they are more like a word-processing typeface than handwriting, which children need to learn about. If at all possible, it would be good to make your own because you can form the handwritten letters properly. It would also be helpful to have lower and upper case, something that you rarely see in commercial sets.

✪ Provide opportunities for your child to make marks/play at writing.

✪ Teach your child to form the letters (see Chapter 4).

✪ Talk about the names of the letters in your child's name.

✪ Talk about words and the letters in words.

Phonological understanding requires knowledge about letters *and* phonemes. The list above shows things that are particularly helpful when learning letters, and the list on the next page will help with learning phonemes.

✪ Sing as many nursery rhymes and songs as you can remember. Buy nursery-rhyme books, poetry books, song books and other rhyming books. Have fun with the music and dancing. Talk about the way that rhymes work. For example, see if your child can hear the rhyme /il/ in 'Jack and Jill went up the hill'. Ask if they can think of other words that begin with the /j/ sound.

✪ Encourage your child's interest in sounds and music. Talk about the different sounds that you can hear. Encourage them to make sounds and listen to sounds.

✪ Enjoy the repeated sounds of alliteration: five fat sausages sizzling in a pan. Make up lists of words that share the same sound.

✪ Encourage your child to make marks and play at writing. Show them how you write words and sentences. Talk to them about the sounds that the letters and groups of letters make.

✪ When reading with your child, encourage them to sound out words that they're not sure of. If they struggle with this at first, sound the word out for them to see if they recognize it.

✪ Use magnetic letters to link with the sounds of words. For example, as you and your child say the sounds in the word, see if they can find the appropriate letters.

✪ Talk about the sounds that are represented by words in the environment.

✪ Write your child's name and talk about the sounds in the word. Do the same for other family and friends' names. Do the same with words for familiar objects.

✪ Draw words in a frame with boxes that show the way that letters represent the phonemes (see the example on the next page).

These kinds of activities and discussions are enough to allow most children to gain the phonological knowledge they need to help them learn to decode words before they start school. However, some children do require more systematic approaches (see the section *What is phonics?* on page 77).

Here's an example of a phoneme frame (some words arranged in phonemes):

m	o	th	er

th	r	ough

g	r	a	ss

Phonemes of word:

/m/ /u/ /th/ /u/

/th/ /r/ /ue/

/g/ /r/ /a/ /s/
**(for those in the north
of England)**
/g/ /r/ /ar/ /s/
**(for those in the south
of England)**

A model of reading

In order to recognize words visually, children rely on representations of words at three levels: meaning (*semantic*); sounds (*phonology*) and spelling (*orthography*). Your child needs these three levels to work together.

Semantic level

If you take the semantic representation of words, it can be helpful to ask, 'Does that make sense?' about something they've read. Encouraging your child to read to the end of a sentence and then return to a problem word can help them use the meaning of the sentence to recognize a particular word. If they substitute a different word from the one printed in the text, then asking, 'Is that right?' encourages them to think about the meaning of what they have been reading and to confirm whether the guess they made is accurate. In general terms, here are things you can do to help your child to use semantic representations:

✪ **Talk to them about the meaning of what they're reading.**
✪ **Ask questions like: 'What do you think is going to happen next?'
or 'What's the story so far?' or 'Why did they do that?' (talking about characters).**
✪ **In fact, any conversation that requires understanding the meaning of the text helps to underline for your child that semantics is an important part of their reading.**

My advice to use real texts, rather than placing too much emphasis on words out of context (like single words on cards, called *flashcards*), also supports your child's learning of the semantic level of word recognition.

Orthographic level

Awareness of orthographic representations is helped by looking at chunks of words. For example, you can help your child to see words broken down into syllables so that they can read one syllable, then another. Prefixes and suffixes are a useful part of this. If you take the word 'play' and add 'ed', you get 'played'. 'ed' can, of course, be added to most verbs (pour**ed**; danc**ed**; act**ed**; plant**ed**; paint**ed**) although this suffix will sound different, depending on the word: either /ed/ or /d/; act-/**ed**/ as opposed to play-/**d**/. If you add 're' to the beginning of play, you get 'replay'. The prefix 're' can also be added to many words (**re**pair; **re**act; **re**ward; **re**ply). This idea of using spelling patterns as chunks of words is important because research shows that one of the strategies that helps children learn to read is called 'reading by analogy'. For example, if you know the word 'pink' then this helps you recognize words like 'ink', 'link', 'stink' and so on. The analogies don't have to sound the same, so patterns like 'ough' in words like 'ought', 'through' and 'rough' are also part of this strategy.

Phonological level

Using the phonological representation of words is particularly important at this stage. Some researchers say that children need to appreciate two special types of sounds before they move on to individual phonemes. If you divide a word into syllables, then a syllable has an *onset* and a *rime*. No, I haven't spelled that wrongly, it really is *rime*. The onset is the first consonant or consonants of a syllable, and the rime is the remaining vowels and consonants of the syllable. Here are some examples:

Example of word	Syllable	Onset	Rime
clang	clang	cl---	--ang
out	out	no onset	out
running	*first syllable*: run	r--	-un

Children also need help to understand phonemes. At the most basic level, the question 'Can you sound it out?' encourages your child to attempt to work out what phonemes the letters of a problem word make. Many children struggle with identifying phonemes. In fact, my experience of training teachers shows that it's not that easy for adults either! If your child struggles to even attempt to sound out a word, you can help:

✪ **Say the phonemes in a word which they can repeat after you.**
✪ **Then you can see if they can blend the sounds together to get the word. Let's say that the word is 'you'. This word has two phonemes /y/ and /ue/. If the word is 'inside', its five phonemes are /i/ /n/ /s/ /ie/ /d/.**
✪ **Once your child has succeeded in working out a tricky word, it's often a good idea to ask them to go back to the start of the sentence and read it again so that they don't lose the flow of meaning.**
✪ **At other times, it may be better if they just continue reading to avoid too much repetition and stopping-and-starting.**

Knowing when to keep the flow of reading going, and when to intervene, is something you'll learn as you get used to helping your child. When your child succeeds in doing this, they will begin to commit more and more whole words to memory. These become part of the 'sight vocabulary', which enables quicker recognition of words and more fluent reading.

What is phonics?

Phonics is an approach to teaching reading which emphasizes the *systematic* teaching of phonemes and their associated letters. You may also have heard the terms *synthetic phonics* and *analytic phonics*. Synthetic phonics emphasizes learning the phonemes by pronouncing them in *isolation* from words and sentences. Analytic phonics emphasizes learning phonemes by analysing words into their syllables, onsets and rimes (see opposite), and phonemes. Despite frequent exaggerated claims in favour of *synthetic* phonics, research shows that all *systematic* phonics approaches are effective in supporting decoding.

In Early Years and infant settings, phonics teaching is done more systematically than you need to do it at home.

✪ **Don't feel you have to teach phonics. I would re-emphasize that it's not usually necessary because your child will be able to crack the code as long as you provide the kinds of support explained in this book.**

There has been much research into phonics, but one of the things it has not been able to tell us is the best sequence for teaching the phonemes. My view is that there won't be a definitive answer to this. Once children start to make the connections themselves, having been taught some of the phonemes, the exact sequence becomes less important because they start learning independently.

Reading aloud and reading silently

Once children can decode efficiently, their sight-vocabulary (words they recognize quickly from memory) rapidly increases, leading to ever-greater fluency. During this stage, even when your child is reading on their own, you'll hear them reading the words quietly to themselves, something called *sub-vocalising*. Increasingly, though, with the fluency that comes from sight-words, they'll move towards reading silently. This is another important milestone on the way to becoming a reader. Incidentally, just in case you think that you never read out loud to yourself, think back to reading a text that was really difficult for you, perhaps one with unknown terminology and concepts. You may have found that you spontaneously reverted to sounding words out!

There comes a point with most children when reading a story aloud to them at bedtime is not necessary because they're reading independently.

✪ **In order to bridge the stage between you reading aloud and your child reading silently, a very good approach is to share the reading, perhaps where you read one page and your child reads the next page, or by sharing out the voices of the characters and narrator.**

Children often enjoy this more active kind of reading.

It can also give you an opportunity to listen to the kind of vocal expression that they use. Being able to provide appropriate expression when reading aloud is a demanding skill because you need to read *ahead* of the point in the text that you are reading. Let me illustrate this. Here's a very short extract from the outstanding book *Holes*, by Louis Sachar, which is probably most appropriate for children aged ten or older.

Stanley could see some kids dressed in orange and carrying shovels dragging themselves toward the tents.

"You thirsty?" asked Mr Sir.

"Yes, Mr Sir," Stanley said gratefully.

"Well, you better get used to it. You're going to be thirsty for the next eighteen months."

If you're reading this aloud with a child, they could play Stanley, the boy, and you could perhaps play Mr Sir, the guard in the Camp Green Lake Juvenile Correction Facility. You would both know from reading the

earlier parts of the book who the two characters are and what they are like. In order to use the appropriate intonation for Stanley's reply, 'Yes, Mr Sir,' the reader has to see the word 'gratefully' and quickly process this information to decide what Stanley's voice might sound like before reading Stanley's answer. This is why reading aloud for performances can be useful because it requires a full understanding and interpretation of the text to be translated into more dramatic reading.

The time when reading aloud to your child naturally comes to an end often coincides with the point at which your child does nearly all of their reading silently. By this time they are fluent readers who will gradually progress through more and more demanding texts. In one sense it can be a slightly sad moment because the shared experience of reading stories together is one of the joys of parenthood.

At the same time, it marks another small rite of passage towards independence, so should be celebrated. However, there are some parents and children who continue to read aloud well into the teenage years because the shared experience is so important to them.

It's worth remembering that although listening to your child reading out loud gives a pretty good understanding of their reading development, it's not exactly the same as their reading silently. For some children, their reading out loud does not match their silent reading. This is particularly the case for quiet children who don't much like the slightly performance aspect of reading out loud. Teachers get round this by encouraging older children to read an extract of text silently and then talk to the teacher about it.

✪ **At this crucial stage of development, you need to listen to your child reading aloud because it enables you to give the most appropriate support to help them improve.**

Expectations for reading age four to seven

What you can expect	What you can do to help
Silent reading established.	Provide time, space, opportunities and resources to encourage your child to read at any time.
Can accurately read increasing number of unknown texts independently.	Ensure that your child has access to 'new' books on a regular basis. The local library can be an excellent resource for this. Buy some books that your child can keep in their collection. Share the kinds of texts that you read, such as newspapers, recipe books, internet information, etc. Subscribe to a comic or magazine for your child.
Uses expression when reading aloud.	Have fun with using expression when you are reading to your child. Encourage your child to read at a good speed and with expression when they share books with you. If your child is involved in any kind of performance where they have to read out loud, such as a class assembly at school, help them with expression and clarity.
Uses a range of word-reading strategies appropriately.	Help your child to use semantic, phonological and orthographic knowledge to work out tricky words. Praise them for good guesses and supply the correct word if necessary.
Stronger individual preferences for particular texts.	Encourage your child to develop preferences for particular topics and types of texts.
Likes reading longer stories in addition to returning to picture books.	Provide access to books with more text and fewer pictures.
Sight-word reading for rapidly increasing bank of familiar words.	The more your child reads, the more sight-words they will acquire.
Phonological knowledge fully established. Growing awareness of irregularities of English spelling.	Help your child to see that the one-letter-makes-one-sound idea is not accurate. Discuss the irregularities of English spelling.

age seven to eleven

What kind of books do *you* like?

The task of guiding your child's reading from seven onwards is quite different from the task of helping them from the ages of four to seven. At the start of the seven-to-11 age group, books are still relatively short so you can read them quickly and evaluate their quality. But by the time children are 11 they tend to be reading short novels. The difficulty for parents and others involved with children is having time to read such books. Fortunately, this is not so necessary at this stage. Your child will develop their own preferences for reading which they will follow, just as adults do. Books will be recommended to them at school and by their friends. However, you will still be able to influence your child's reading by the interest you take in it, your own recommendations, and through the books you buy for them.

Wonderful books

Towards the end of this stage, the distinction between books for children and books for adults begins to break down. Among the distinctive features of literature for young people in recent years has been its crossover appeal. One of the most famous is the *Harry Potter* series by J. K. Rowling. In the early days of their release, there were two different book jackets, one for children and a more boring-looking one for adults. Another example of a popular crossover book is *The Curious Incident of the Dog in the Night-Time*, which features a central character who is a child, yet the events that lead to the curious incident consist of the adult themes of adultery and murder. Many children will move on to read books that are aimed directly at adults. I remember my own interest in the James Herbert horror books as a young teenager – don't a sk me why huge killer rats, swarms of bees, or tidal waves submerging London interested me!

The book I've chosen to exemplify wonderful writing for children in this age-range is *Skellig*, by David Almond.[1] The plot focuses on something that a boy called Michael finds at the back of the dilapidated garage that's part of the house he has just moved into. I won't tell you what this is because it would spoil the story! The other plot line concerns the health of Michael's baby sister who has a heart problem. Throughout the book, Almond portrays Michael's uncertainties and worries about his sister in the most authentic and touching way. Towards the end of the

book, Michael's sister recovers from an operation and mum and the baby
return home:

> *'Welcome home, Mum,' I whispered, using the words I'd*
> *practised.*
>
> *She smiled at how nervous I was. She took my hand*
> *and led me back into the house, into the kitchen. She sat*
> *me on a chair and put the baby in my arms.*
>
> *'Look how beautiful your sister is,' she said. 'Look*
> *how strong she is.'*
>
> *I lifted the baby higher. She arched her back as*
> *if she was about to dance or fly. She reached out, and*
> *scratched with her tiny nails at the skin on my face. She*
> *tugged at my lips and touched my tongue. She tasted of*
> *milk and salt and of something mysterious, sweet and*
> *sour all at once. She whimpered and gurgled. I held her*
> *closer and her dark eyes looked right into me, right into*
> *the place where all my dreams were, and she smiled.*
>
> *'She'll have to keep going for check-ups,' Mum said.*
> *'But they're sure the danger's gone, Michael. Your sister is*
> *really going to be all right.'*
>
> *We laid the baby on the table and sat around her.*
> *We didn't know what to say. Mum drank her tea. Dad let*
> *me have swigs of his beer. We just sat there looking at*
> *each other and touching each other and we laughed and*
> *laughed and we cried and cried.*[2]

The use of language in this passage is exquisite. The human senses
of sight, touch, smell and taste overwhelm us. The image of the view
through the eyes to 'the place where all my dreams were' is striking. The
profound relief about the baby's escape from death is made more poignant
by the seemingly mundane language of 'swigs' of beer.

Skellig is good for children of nine or ten onwards because it's a
gripping story. But like all the best children's literature it also encourages
a greater depth of thought in its readers through its recurring themes. Its
main theme is a celebration of life, but this is contrasted with exploration
about what happens to things when they die. Another theme concerns

learning and education. Michael meets a new friend called Mina. One of their discussions is about owls and Almond uses the opportunity to present factual information about owls in the guise of the children's curiosity. During another one of their conversations, we hear Mina's description of her learning. This section reveals some of Almond's beliefs:

> *'My mother educates me,' she said. 'We believe that schools inhibit the natural curiosity, creativity and intelligence of children. The mind needs to be opened out into the world, not shuttered down inside a gloomy classroom.'*

Hear, hear!

Almond's work has popular appeal but is distinctly literary. For example, in addition to the themes that are addressed, he makes explicit reference to the work of William Blake. There can be a great deal of snobbery attached to literary texts. Now, I'm not arguing that such texts are unimportant. Of course they are and, personally, I'd like to see all children access texts that are generally regarded as classics. But snobbery is frequently a factor when people insist that children read particular types of books rather than others, so my advice is:

✪ **Allow children to read what interests them most. Don't feel they must read 'classic' books if they're not keen. They should develop preferences and pursue them in ever-greater depth. Your role as parent is to discuss with interest what your children read and sometimes seek to persuade them of the possibilities of other kinds of texts.**

✪ **At this stage, don't worry about what they read as long as they read something.**

Multimedia

Another example of the kind of snobbery I've just mentioned is the idea that reading the book is somehow intrinsically better than watching the film. Although I'm not the sort of technophile that says the book is about to be replaced by electronic alternatives, I do think that multimedia is of growing importance to children's learning. Although there are potential dangers inherent in this explosion of multimedia, the advantages far outweigh them. Apart from anything else, it would be counter-productive and futile to try to stop children accessing these media.

✪ **Try to engage with your child's interest in multimedia, even if you lack confidence in your own IT skills. Multimedia is a feature of your child's world and an important aspect of their learning today.**

Here's an example of the way that film played a positive part in Olly's reading. Olly was seven when the first film in the *Lord of the Rings* trilogy opened, so I was reluctant to take him to see it because of the violent nature of many scenes. Eventually, I decided to buy the DVD so that I could sit with him while we watched, make sure he was OK and talk to him about the film. Some might say that even this mediated viewing was inappropriate but, as the subsequent films were viewed at the cinema, the whole experience led to a rich seam of development for Olly: role-play using his bow and arrows from York's Jorvik Centre and his *Harry Potter* sword with sound effects; dramatic re-enactment with toy models of the characters; defeat of Orcs, Uruk-Hai and other unpleasant monsters on the Sony Playstation *Lord of the Rings* game; and all of these in the context of sustained motivation, interest and determination. Olly also made a very good attempt (for a seven-year-old) to read *The Fellowship*

of the Ring, which quite quickly resulted in him skimming and scanning to find his favourite bits.

My own interest in the book was rekindled, along with slight guilt that I still hadn't read one of the greatest pieces of literature for young people, so, having not enjoyed the books as a teenager, I tried again and was transfixed. Many interesting conversations followed where Olly and I compared our understandings of the film and print versions of *The Fellowship*. Olly's factual knowledge of characters and particular details remained greater than mine but, because he didn't read all of *The Fellowship*, he had less understanding of where, for example, the film differed from the books. The point of telling you this story is to say that films are one important type of 'text' available for children. Films can also be an excellent introduction and complement to books that children might not otherwise read.

An example of imaginative use of media in book form is *The Adventures of Super Diaper Baby,*[3] a book which may have influenced Olly's writing style in 'Little Dead Riding Hood' (see Chapter 6). The book is a graphic story which is an important form internationally, but one which is often neglected in English schools. The first section explains how the writers were in trouble at school and were made to do some writing as a punishment, but they were not allowed to write the story of *Captain Underpants* again, so they came up with *Super Diaper Baby*. The language of the book is packed with jokes and games. Apart from the deliberately self-aware opening which explains the school context as if real, there are also other genre tricks. There are information sections which tell you how to draw the main characters and explanations about how to enjoy 'flip-o-rama' (flicker book images), which is an ingenious way of introducing moving images in a printed text.

> *FLIP-O-RAMA 8*
> *Remember, flip only page 77. You know, since nobody reads these pages, we figured they'd be a good place to insert subliminal messages:*
> *Think for yourself. Question Authority. Read banned books! Kids have the same constitutional rights as grown-ups!!!*
> *Don't forget to boycott standardized testing!!!*[4]

I couldn't agree more with the final sentence there, but more about the statutory tests at the end of this chapter. The book is written colloquially and includes the kinds of spelling and grammatical originality that a child writer might use:

> *Our story Begins as a caR is speding to the Hospital.*
> *Hurry up! I'm Hurry Upping!*

The table on the next page shows some more books that I recommend when your child is this age.

Books that help you find books

I offer this section instead of the Top Ten lists I offered in the first two chapters on reading. A good solution to the problem of knowing enough children's books for this age range is to use guides to children's books. *The Ultimate Book Guide*,[5] covering books for children aged eight to 12, is a very good example.

A frequent cry from Olly was, 'I don't know what to read', or 'All my books are boring!' (even though he hadn't read them all!). As part of my work I'd come across *The Ultimate Book Guide* and had been reading it at home. I showed it to Olly. The thing that surprised me most was that Olly enjoyed reading the book guide itself, for pleasure, because it features short text extracts about books and includes some front covers to look at.

Just to give you a flavour of the information, here's an extract about *The Princess Diaries*, by Meg Cabot:

> *Just because you've seen the movie, don't deny yourself*
> *this treat. Like all the best children's fiction, this series*
> *can be enjoyed by adults as well as kids.*
> *Brilliantly written in the form of an ongoing diary*
> *with lots of fun pop culture references, these books*
> *are delectable! Mia Thermopolis is fourteen when she*
> *discovers that her Jean-Luc-Picard-lookalike father is*
> *really the crowned prince of a small European country.*
> *And as his only daughter, she is a princess!*
> *Meg Cabot makes you feel you really know what*

being a high school student in New York is like. And besides being funny, well-written and totally unputdownable, this book has lots of delightful lists. For example, here is a list of Mia's favourite books: IQ 83, Jaws, The Catcher in the Rye, To Kill a Mockingbird *and* A Wrinkle in Time *('only we never get to find out the most important thing: whether or not Meg has breasts ...')*

REVIEWED BY CAROLINE LAWRENCE
RECOMMENDED AGE: 10+

Using the internet

The internet has a huge range of information about books, not least from publishers who are finding increasingly imaginative ways to market their books. An innovative review site which was started by children, for children, is Cool Reads. Two boys started the site when they were 13 and 11. The site now features many reviews from readers around the world.

On page 92 you can see one of the reviews from this site. It was written by Tim from the Cool Reads team. Tim wrote this review when he was 15 years old.

Books for children aged seven to 11

Type of book	Example
Classic story	*The Iron Man*, by Ted Hughes
Story with difficult issues for characters	*The Illustrated Mum*, by Jacqueline Wilson
Combination of comic book and standard narrative	*Captain Underpants and the Attack of the Talking Toilets*, by Dav Pilkey
Modern American literature	*Holes* by Louis Sachar
Classic non-fiction format	*Star Wars Attack of the Clones, the Visual Dictionary*, by David West Reynolds
Innovative non-fiction format	*Horrid Histories: The Terrible Tudors*, by Terry Deary and Neil Tonge
Poetry	*There's an awful lot of weirdos in our neighbourhood*, by Colin McNaughton
Traditional tales from other countries	*Seasons of Splendour*, by Madhur Jaffrey
Larger-scale format	*A Street Through Time*, illustrated by Steve Noon and written by Anne Millard

Why is it good?	Any limitations?	By same author
A gripping story told in language that is simple but poetic. One of the best opening pages of a children's book that I have read.	None	N/A
Moving and thought-provoking portrayal of a child's difficult life. Prolific author whose texts often engender powerful emotions.	Probably more likely to appeal to girls.	*Candyfloss*
Zany, funny and inventive. Definite appeal to boys. Features 'flip-o-rama'!	Comic book features and toilet humour may not appeal to all.	*Captain Underpants and the Preposterous Plight of the Purple Potty People*
A unique voice and one of the best pieces of children's literature I have read. Very clever plot with mysteries to solve.	None	*Someday Angeline*
Dorling Kindersley's *Eye Witness Guide* format was groundbreaking when it first came out. These books, in the same format, link with the *Star Wars* films and are intriguing because they are factual books about a fictional subject.	Quite heavy on text and a demanding read.	*Kennedy Space Center: Gateway to Space*
Brilliant way to make history fun and funny. The books now have many imitators.	A demanding read which occasionally pitches the level too high for this age group.	*Flight of the Fire Thief*
A book of modern poetry that is not an anthology and really works as a whole. Funny and clever.	Not profound poetry, but not meant to be.	*Football Crazy*
The best example of a collection of traditional tales from another country that I have come across.	Unfamiliar context may not appeal to all.	*Robi Dobi: The Marvelous Adventures of an Indian Elephant*
Shows the same 'street' through a 12 000-year period. The period immediately after the Romans is startling.	None	*A Port Through Time*

Gangsta Rap *by Benjamin Zephaniah*
Bloomsbury, 2004, 333 pages, ISBN 0747565651

How easy was it to get stuck into this book? Gangsta Rap
follows three young people, Ray, Prem and Tyrone, who
won't fit into their lives at all, and whose only aim is to
form a rap band in the future. It charts their rise to fame
and how they deal with all sorts of problems, such as
threatening rival bands and stubborn parents, and is
actually quite engaging and interesting to read.
Who are the main characters? *The main characters are*
the three young drop-outs, Ray, Prem and Tyrone, who
have a very bleak future ahead of them if their lives
continue as they are now. However, they are installed in
a special centre designed to help them with the help of the
school headmaster, Mr Lang, and their dream begins to
come true. Other important characters are Marga Man
(a nickname) who runs the music shop where the boys
spend most of their time, the families of the boys and the
Western Alliance, another rap band which is constantly
challenging the boys' band, often with violence.
What's the storyline? *Following their introduction into the*
centre, the dream soon starts to take place, and the band,
which they call Positive Negatives, is born. However their
rise to fame attracts all sorts of unwelcome attention, and
another band, the Western Alliance is openly scornful and
abusive towards them. This in turn launches a gang war
between the fans of the different bands, and the prospects
for the band seem rather bleak.
How's it written? *Many of the characters in the book speak*
differently, but this doesn't really make any difference to
the book's readability.
Other books by the same author that Tim knows about?
Refugee Boy *and* Face.
The overall verdict is Really good stuff.

Let's talk about books

In the first two phases of your child's development as a reader, birth to age four and four to seven, the focus is mainly on learning to read. This changes, in the phase from seven to 11, to reading to learn. You'll no longer need to help them as much with the mechanics of reading words, but your involvement will be particularly helpful if you talk to them regularly about their reading. Let's imagine that your child has gone to bed and is reading before going to sleep. Although you wouldn't want to interrupt every day, here are some good questions to use:

✪ **Ask 'What are you reading?', followed by, 'Is it any good?'.**
✪ **A more specific question like 'What's happening in the story?' can be a good way to open a conversation about reading.**

Another good opportunity for talking about reading is to take your child to the library or a bookshop. One thing that can be useful if they don't have strong ideas of their own about which book to choose, is to help them understand how to judge quickly if a book is going to be right, by doing things such as these:

✪ **Look at the front cover picture and title – are they interesting?**
✪ **Read the blurb on the back of the book.**
✪ **Try reading a little bit of the first page.**
✪ **Scan various pages throughout the book looking for things of interest. Skim-read small sections for the same reason.**
✪ **Select the book and/or move on to another book and repeat.**

There are many topics that you can talk about with your child in relation to books that they're reading. Think about the kinds of conversations you have with friends about books and see if similar discussions could be initiated with your child on topics such as:

✪ Likes and dislikes.
✪ Top five books.
✪ Memorable moments and aspects of books.
✪ The ways that books relate to real life.
✪ Authors and their work.
✪ Types of books and their features.

- ✪ Conflict in books.
- ✪ Relationships in books.
- ✪ The extent to which information is true.
- ✪ The way that books become dated.
- ✪ Comparisons between print and film.
- ✪ Reading between the lines (see below).

Reading between the lines

One of the important changes in your child's reading at this stage is for them to move from the literal interpretation of texts towards being able to 'read between the lines'. If you think about it, reading *between* the lines is a funny expression. Between the lines there is only space. Actually, all the meanings are contained *within* the lines, it's just the way that you interpret them that changes. What we're really talking about here is the myriad ways that people can interpret texts. Some theorists go so far as to say that there's no fixed interpretation of a text. Each reader decides the meaning through their own interpretation and response. The important thing in relation to the support that you can give your child is that your conversations should encourage interpretation of the texts that they read and, ultimately, the ability to argue a case for their interpretation by referring directly to aspects of the text.

In school, children learn that a product of reading between the lines is *inference* and *deduction*. As the following quotes from the *Oxford English Dictionary* show, it's difficult to differentiate clearly between the two terms, so I'm going to stick with inference.

> Inference
> **1. a.** *The action or process of inferring; the drawing of a conclusion from known or assumed facts or statements; esp. in Logic, the forming of a conclusion from data or premises, either by inductive or deductive methods; reasoning from something known or assumed to something else which follows from it; = ILLATION. Also (with pl.), a particular act of inferring; the logical form in which this is expressed.*

Deduction
6. a. *The process of deducing or drawing a conclusion from a principle already known or assumed; spec. in Logic, inference by reasoning from generals to particulars; opposed to INDUCTION.*

You are the role-model

It's helpful if you remember that the reading that you do is a model to your child and try to do the following things:

✪ **If possible, try to find occasional moments when you sit down and read a text of your choice (chance would be a fine thing!) to present a model that you hope your child will adopt.**
✪ **If there are stories in newspapers or magazines that you think might be interesting, show them to your child.**
✪ **Point to the headlines and help your child to read them.**
✪ **Talk about the issues that the articles raise.**

The sports pages are often one of the first parts of a newspaper that children who are interested in football start to look at independently. The *Sunday Times* even produced a section called the *Funday Times* aimed at children.

Some children get so excited by books that they will happily pick one up at any time during the day and read. Esther and Olly used to do this before they were aged seven. After seven, their home reading was done almost exclusively at bedtime. This mirrored their parents' main time for reading books. At first I was a little concerned, but as they remained keen to read on most days at their preferred time, I couldn't logically see any particular problem. One summer holiday shed further light on this. We were abroad with another family and every day the adults felt that a siesta was called for. Funnily enough, the kids were not too keen on sleeping! However, a supply of books that both families had brought with them (and no TV or other screens) ensured that, rather than go to sleep, Esther and Olly chose to read during the day for pretty much the first time for a year or more.

Helping with reading homework

One thing to say straight away is how rare it is for children's homework at this stage to involve the reading of a whole text. For example, it would be possible for a teacher to set a homework task like this:

Choose something at home to read. Talk to one of your family about what you have read. Here are some hints about what to talk about: What kind of text did you choose? Why did you choose it? How good did you think it was? Why? Be prepared to talk about this in the English/literacy lesson on Friday. Make some notes if this will help you to remember.

Or: Ask someone at home to help you select a recipe. Make the food shown in the recipe. Talk about how well the recipe worked.

Or: Find an internet page that covers something that you are interested in. Discuss the page with someone at home so that you are sure you understand everything on the page. Design an information sheet to inform other children in your class. Bring the information sheet to your next English/literacy lesson.

These are good homework tasks because they involve choice, they involve whole texts and they focus on 'doing' and talking. However, the present educational climate has pushed teachers into structuring learning ever more tightly, usually away from whole texts towards work on words and sentences. In fact (as you will see in Chapter 6), the homework that tends to crop up most is the dreaded learning of spelling lists!

Children differ in how much support they want with homework. If they ask for help, you'll obviously provide it. But it's not a good idea in the long term if you end up doing most of the homework for them because they need to become independent learners. One of the most productive things you can do is help your child develop good routines for homework.

✪ **Help them to see the value of not leaving homework until the last minute.**

✪ **Make sure they have the space/equipment to do their homework.**

✪ **Although a desk in a bedroom can be helpful, one of the advantages of doing homework downstairs is that you can see the kind of homework that is being done and take an active interest.**

Homework frequently involves use of the internet. When this activity involves researching topics that are being covered at school, or topics your child is interested in, this can be useful. One of the main areas where children need support is knowing how appropriate the information on a particular internet site is. If the information is at a reading level way beyond the child's level of understanding, they'll need you to explain in your own words what the information means. Some sites are pitched at a good level for children, for example the BBC's schools area, as the BBC has a track record of developing appropriate resources for children.

✪ **One of the most important things that you can do to help with internet-based homework is to encourage your child to rework information in their own words. Simply cutting and pasting from a site results in a low level of learning. If they have to transform the information into their own words and into a new format, it means that they have to *understand* what they have read.**

Reading at school

Increasingly, much of the reading they do will be done at school. The English curriculum in primary schools is very prescriptive and rarely offers children choice. The custom of children having a reading book of their choice to read during a daily quiet reading time was very common before the Literacy Strategy was introduced in 1997. Although some schools continue to see the importance of children's choice over their reading materials, this kind of reading is less common than it used to be. This means that you play an important role in giving your child choice in what they read.

✪ It's vital that you continue to encourage your child's motivation for and interest in reading by making sure they have plenty of opportunities to choose their own reading matter.

✪ Remember that motivation and interest are the things that will turn your child into a life-long reader and drive them through their education, much more than government prescriptions on what must be taught and learned.

Having said that, it's useful if you know something about the kind of English curriculum that your child will follow at school if you are to help them effectively, for example with their homework. The legal requirement for the school curriculum is contained in the National Curriculum. The National Curriculum is an interesting mix of laudable aims and some quite questionable requirements. The following statement appears on the first page of the English section of the National Curriculum:

> *The importance of English*
> *English is a vital way of communicating in school, in public life and internationally. Literature in English is rich and influential, reflecting the experience of people from many countries and times.*
>
> *In studying English pupils develop skills in speaking, listening, reading and writing. It enables them to express themselves creatively and imaginatively and to communicate with others effectively. Pupils learn to*

become enthusiastic and critical readers of stories, poetry
and drama as well as non-fiction and media texts.
The study of English helps pupils understand how
language works by looking at its patterns, structures
and origins. Using this knowledge pupils can choose and
adapt what they say and write in different situations.

This is a powerful set of statements and most people would agree they
are important. The idea that learning and studying English is first and
foremost about communication, and that skills are there to serve this aim
rather than drive the curriculum is admirable. The ideas that English
should be about creativity and imagination and that children should
be enthusiastic are also very important. Unfortunately, the Literacy
curriculum in England since 1997, as a result of the National Literacy
Strategy, has simply not reflected those aims. You might think that
this is an odd state of affairs, where a statutory National Curriculum is
undermined by a non-statutory Literacy Strategy, but such is the nature
of political interference with the Early Years and Primary Curriculum.

There isn't space in this book to discuss the many areas of
learning about reading that your child will engage with at school (for
more information about the English Curriculum, see *Teaching English,*
Language and Literacy by me and Russell Jones).[6] However, you can
find out more about the detail of what your child should be covering in any
particular year group by looking at the Teaching Framework for Literacy
which is available online at the Standards Site (standards.dfes.gov.uk/).

Testing, testing

Overall, though, it's not the National Curriculum which restricts your
child's opportunities, it is the statutory testing system. In this final section
of the chapter, I'm going to explain how the tests for reading at the end
of Key Stage 2 (ages seven to 11) work. Before I do that, I want to make a
plea for abolishing the statutory tests. England's children are tested more
than children in any other European country and, possibly, in the world.
The tests are part of a high-stakes testing regime which puts schools into
league tables which are published each year in the media. The tests serve

very little purpose for your child. They provide some limited information about how your child performed on one day in their life in relation to their peers. However, any good teacher could tell you the same by using their own assessment information. This could include standardized test scores, if a more objective measure were required. Teachers' assessment information is more useful than the statutory tests because they can give specific advice on how to help in the areas where your child is weak, something that the outcomes of the national tests do not do.

The tests also only give very basic information about your child's school. The single most important factor in the outcomes of school test scores is the socio-economic background of the children. Children from more advantaged backgrounds perform better in tests, on average, than those from disadvantaged backgrounds. This has been shown again and again in a wide range of research. A school with high test scores is not necessarily a school that will be the best for your child. Some schools move their pupils forward very effectively, but because the pupils start from a disadvantaged position this is not reflected in the test scores. The attempts to try and show this through what is called a *value added* measure have been misleading, as Stephen Gorard's[7] statistical analysis shows.

It doesn't have to be like this!

In the light of the problems with the statutory tests, Wales has abandoned published league tables of school results. Scotland has always had a system which is more about diagnostically testing children when they are ready. The really damaging aspect of a high-stakes testing regime is that the curriculum for children is narrowed because teachers understandably teach to what is required in the tests as, to a certain extent, their jobs depend on good test scores.

Bill Boyle and Joanna Bragg[8] have clearly shown the way that the focus on tests and targets in mathematics and English since 1997 has dramatically reduced the amount of time that your child spends on all the other subjects. As I go round schools I see lessons dominated by short-term objectives; targets set for children based on their perceived progress towards test scores; and formal testing carried out every year. Education really does not have to be like this, so I urge you to argue for the abolition of the testing system as it currently stands.

About the tests

Right, I'll just climb down off my soapbox so I can give you some information about the tests. This information is based on the tests carried out in 2006. The reading test consists of a booklet that children have to read and a series of questions they have to answer. In 2006, the booklet was called *Heart Beat* and was an information text about drumming that included a short introduction; a short biography about Evelyn Glennie, the world-famous percussionist; some information about drumming around the world; and a section on skills needed to become a drummer. The booklet was in full colour, including photos of drums, other percussion and a variety of performers from around the world. As a text, not bad at all, and something that could interest many children. There will, of course, always be some children who are not in the slightest bit interested in the chosen topic. In this case, despite the picture of a young person playing kit drums on the front cover, the main information was all about the classical percussionist Evelyn Glennie, a topic less likely to appeal to the majority of children than information focusing, say, on pop music. This highlights a big problem with a national testing system as opposed to a system based on teacher assessment. In the national tests one text has to be chosen for all children, whereas children could be assessed reading and responding to a text of their choice if the teacher was doing the assessment. The nature of children's reading differs according to the text they are reading.

Having read the text in the booklet, your child will then have to write answers to questions. The answers have four different formats: short answers of a word or phrase (these include ticking a box as part of multiple choice); several line answers; longer answers which require a more detailed explanation of the pupil's opinion; and other answers which have different requirements. A very worrying aspect of this test is that nearly all the answers are of the kind which require a short answer based on low-level comprehension of the text. Only three of the questions, out of 30, attracted three marks for a correct longer answer. One of these required the completion of missing cells in a table of summary information.

Question 13 was a question which did require inference and a higher level of thought. The booklet explaining the marking criteria includes examples of answers from pupils who trialled the tests (presumably not English pupils!). The following quote follows the layout of the marking criteria booklet.

> **13. Why do you think many people admire Evelyn Glennie?**
> **up to 3 marks**
> **Assessment focus 3: deduce, infer or interpret information, events or ideas from texts (complex inference).**
> **Possible points might refer to Evelyn's:**
> - **musical ability**
> - **sensory ability**
> - **determination/perseverance**
> - **professional success**
> - **inspiration to others**
>
> **Award 3 marks for answers which provide substantial coverage of at least two points, e.g.:**
> - **I think many people admire her because she is such a talented person and she can sense the notes through her body and it is very interesting, almost as if she is psychic. Also many people may just learn from her example (sensory ability and inspiration)**
>
> **Award 2 marks for answers which either explore one of the points above in more detail/with textual support or explore two of the points superficially, e.g.:**
> - **because she is a great musician and also because she can't hear but she still performs and plays successfully (musical ability and determination)**
>
> **Award 1 mark for answers which are either very general or refer to a very specific detail relating to one of the points above, e.g.:**
> - **she gives around 110 concerts a year (success)**

In the light of this, the obvious advice to help your child succeed in the reading test would be: ask them lots of short, specific comprehension questions about texts that they read. The problem with this advice is that it's a very unnatural form of questioning. It's also very limited and might actually detract from deeper forms of thought. The sort of questions that you should be asking are the kinds that I covered in the section above, *Let's talk about books* (page 93). This brings me back to my criticism of the tests in general; they are not assessing many of the things that are important in terms of your child's learning.

Expectations for reading at age 11

What you can expect	What you can do to help
Reflective reader with strong preferences.	Discuss texts that your child is reading and seek to extend their understanding of the issues raised.
Uses different reading styles for different texts.	Encourage your child to become involved with things like map-reading or locating information on the internet.
Can follow instructional texts.	Do some cooking together which requires use of a recipe book. Involve your child in following instructions to assemble things (some might say this was cruelty, if it was flat-pack furniture!)
Can sort and classify evidence.	Support your child's homework.
Varies pace, pitch and expression when reading aloud, and varies for performance purposes.	Discuss occasions when your child has to perform. Encourage involvement in dramatic activities at home and at school.
Can adopt alternative viewpoints.	The starting point for this might be the ability to empathize with others. Encourage consideration of evidence from different sides of an argument.
Recognizes language devices used for particular effects.	Enjoy the imagination of authors who like to play with text effects. Re-read texts such as poetry to discover effects.
Can discuss different author styles.	Encourage children to read lots of books by the authors that they like and to think about their style.
Enjoys selecting and reading appropriate adult texts.	Encourage access to newspapers and magazines.

birth to age four

Yes, you can write with a baby!

The physical and mental attributes required for reading and writing begin to develop very early in your child's life. As you saw in the chapter about reading from birth to four, the first significant reading experience happens when your child is about three months old. An important difference between reading and writing is that writing requires the ability to make a mark. This could be a mark made with a finger in sand or with finger-paint on paper. But at some point the child needs to develop the fine motor control that enables them to grasp a writing implement. This motor control is a skill that develops a little later than the ability to play with a book or listen to stories. This is not to say that reading and writing development are completely separate. On the contrary, all the aspects that are a feature of reading from birth to four will have a beneficial impact on writing from birth to four, and vice versa.

When Esther was one year old, we recorded that she made her first marks on paper with a writing implement. At 1y 10m she was beginning to realize that she could communicate meaning through pictures. At breakfast time one morning she said, 'Cow,' in relation to a drawing that she had done. One of us misheard her and asked her if she had said 'Car,' to which she replied, 'Yeah!' This might seem strange to you. How could a cow be a car? The important thing is that Esther had realized that pictures could carry meanings. However, she didn't yet understand that the meaning of a picture is permanent once it is finished.

This idea of the permanence of meaning applies to both pictures and print and is one of the important things that children have to learn. When Esther was 2y 1m, she started to draw what she called a 'tick tock' but, by the time she had finished, she said it was a 'banana' because it did look more like one than a clock. Her understanding had moved on: she understood that the meaning of pictures is permanent. So if she drew something that looked more like a banana, then it was a banana, even if it began life as a clock! Her understanding that print carries meaning was shown in the same month, when she saw a shopping list and asked, 'What does it say?' At 2y 3m we read a letter from Grandma to Esther and encouraged her to write a reply. She drew several diagonal lines which ran from left to right and said that it meant 'I would like one'. We suggested some other sentences that she might write. Her signature was represented by some smaller lines that she drew.

A first written masterpiece

In Chapter 1, I drew your attention to the important role that nursery rhymes play in young children's development. Both Esther and Olly had wide exposure to nursery rhymes, including singing them with us, listening to audio CDs, reading them in books, seeing them and hearing them on TV, joining in at their play group and nursery, playing with nursery-rhyme cards, and so on. In this chapter, I want to share one example of Olly engaging with *writing* a nursery rhyme when he was 4y 9m. Early one morning he came and sat on the floor in our bedroom. He had a pencil and a sheet of paper. You can see what he wrote below.

Olly's writing

Can you work out the nursery rhyme that he was writing? (Answer at the bottom of the page.) The video clip of him doing this writing shows a remarkable period of extended concentration. You can see that he had a particular readership in mind: the members of his family. You can also see the wonderful use of invented spelling: wns (once); wiy (why); yooh (you); bcos (because). This shows the way that talking feeds into writing, but also how they are such different forms of language.

Scribe for your child

It helps if you think about the writing process as consisting of two major areas: *composition* and *transcription*. The writer has to *compose* the ideas for the writing but also has to have the skills to *transcribe* (write down) these ideas as text. One is the authorship side and the other is the secretarial side. Frequently it helps to separate these two sides during the process of writing. This applies to all writers, not just children. Having spent months working mainly on the composition of this book, attention turned to the secretarial details such as particular use of words, spelling and so on. In fact, the separation between composition and transcription is made clearer by the fact that copy editors and proof readers help with the transcription.

1, 2, 3, 4, 5, Once I caught a fish alive.

✪ One really good way to support composition and relieve the burden of transcription is if you act as scribe (or secretary) for your child's ideas.

✪ When you scribe for your child, they give you as many of the ideas as possible and you write them down using their language.

✪ By using your child's language you are making clear links between spoken and written words. They can hear the idea in speech then see it being written. It's important, at this stage, to use your child's language even if it is grammatically 'incorrect'.

At this point I'd like to introduce the term *unconventional* rather than 'incorrect' in relation to your child's writing. Your child is learning about the English writing system which is full of conventions. These conventions have developed through the history of our language. When children try to write, their attempts are always logical and, increasingly, will get closer to conventional English. Simply to view their early attempts as incorrect is not to take into account the incredible logical thought that accompanies their efforts to learn to write, and is a reflection of low expectations of your child's ability.

✪ When you scribe for your child, it helps if you establish a topic and a format first. One format I'd highly recommend is bookmaking.

The first time I wrote a book with Esther she was 2y 11m. I told her that we were going to write a story together and that we would make it into a book. Sometimes I prompted her with ideas and questions and, at other times, I simply wrote down the words that she said. I wrote the first draft of the story onto a sheet of paper. Next, it was transcribed onto the computer. I left spaces between chunks of the text so that they could be printed out, cut up and stuck onto the different pages of the book. Finally, I encouraged Esther to draw pictures to match the text on each page. See what Esther's finished book looked like on the next two pages.

When you involve your child in this process of cutting and pasting, it's a good opportunity to re-read the chunks of text with them and make decisions about the order of pages. This kind of text-matching and text-sorting activity is very helpful for reading as well as writing.

WALK IN THE JUNGLE

WRITTEN BY ESTHER WISE

Esther was going to the jungle. She saw the moon in the sky.

1.

All of a sudden she heard a strange noise. When she turned round she saw a dinosaur. The dinosaur was called Turtle Turtle.
He said "Zenga Zenga" to Esther.
Esther said "Dadda Dadda"

2.

Another dinosaur heard them talking and came to have a look. She was followed by a third dinosaur.

3.

Esther's first book (continues on next page)

Esther and the dinosaur had a dance that went bounce, bounce, bounce.

Esther Ruth saw the sun coming up so she knew she had to go home.

4.

5.

Esther's first book (continued)

It's not just scribble!

Many people might look at the marks that a child of, say, two has made and conclude that it is 'just scribble'. This would be far from the truth. The marks that your child makes in the very earliest stages are a genuine attempt to communicate meaning. As in all aspects of their life, they are actively exploring. The problem for adults is that your child is not using conventional writing.

✪ **You should always assume that your child intends to communicate meaning.**

✪ **Ask them about their writing and respond to what they say.**

The study that Jerome Harste[1] and his colleagues carried out gave a very good example of how to look positively at children's mark-making. The children in their study were three- and four-year-olds. One of the children in the study had developed more slowly than the other children in her nursery. She puzzled the researchers and at first they found it difficult to

see the positive aspects of her writing. It would have been easy to dismiss
Latrice's writing as mere scribble. But, after much work with Latrice, the
researchers were able to give a positive account.

✪ Latrice was aware of how to use writing implements and paper.

✪ She understood and demonstrated the difference between writing and
pictures.

✪ She switched between writing and drawing as a strategy to maintain
the flow of her writing. This made it hard for people to know which of her
marks were drawing and which were writing at any one time in the process.

✪ Each new mark represented a new or different idea. An important aspect
of writing is that each mark (e.g. letter or word) has a distinct and different
meaning. This is an important thing to learn. Most children will go though a
phase where they use the same letter for more than one meaning.

✪ She had some knowledge of the importance of space in relation to text.

✪ She was aware of the permanence of meaning in relation to written
language.

Before they understand that the meaning of writing and pictures is
permanent, children will give you different accounts at different times of
what their marks mean. If you can be with them as they actually make the
marks, you'll be able to engage with their originally-intended meaning.
These conversations are an ideal opportunity to help improve their writing.

✪ **It's important to talk to your child about their drawing and
writing, not only at the end but also during the process of writing.**

Writing stuff

Here are three basic things you can do to encourage your child to write:

- ✪ **Provide writing resources that are within easy reach of your child.**
- ✪ **Provide a good variety of resources, for everyday and 'special' use.**
- ✪ **Make sure there's plenty of space to write in.**

One of the best ways to help your child's writing is to provide resources that they can access themselves. There are two main sorts of resource: everyday materials and occasional materials. For everyday use you need a good stock of paper. It can be recycled paper, perhaps from computer printouts or blank sheets. Varying kinds of pads, including lined and blank paper, are also useful. And, of course, writing implements: lots of pencils with good tips; plenty of black felt-pens with washable ink. Once your child understands that pens such as biros don't wash off clothes and walls, they'll come in handy, too. A good set of pencil crayons and one of high-quality, coloured felt-tips are also valuable for drawings.

Occasional materials include better-quality paper for 'special' work; simple booklets that can be made by folding and stapling sheets of paper; special coloured papers; coloured card; art materials; printing blocks; wax crayons, and so on. These resources are best kept for occasional use as they are more expensive and can be wasted. This separation between everyday materials and special materials can also be linked to the idea of different drafts of writing. Early drafts are done on ordinary paper, but presentation or final drafts are made using higher-quality materials. Young children take some time to appreciate the value of different materials. Children also need space – possibly on a convenient table, but quite often on the floor is best. Although the untidiness can be inconvenient, it's important that they have plenty of space to write.

I can write my ABC

In Chapter 2, I explained how full understanding of the alphabet and its letters is one of the great challenges for children. Here, I focus on another part of this understanding: how to form the letters. Before I go into the detail, it's a good idea if you understand some of the key principles

involved in helping children's handwriting. Rosemary Sassoon's[2] work on handwriting is excellent so I draw on her ideas a great deal here (and in later handwriting sections). Ultimately, the goal for your child is a legible, fluent and comfortable handwriting style.

The direction of writing is crucial (this is related to the orientation of texts discussed in Chapter 1), as are the specific movements of the pen (or other writing implement) and the particular heights of lines and letters. Letters are made by conventional movements with specific starting points and exit points. Letters also have particular height differences.

Speed – but not too much speed – is also important as this leads to fluency and greater efficiency. Exams and tests are one example of when you need to think and write reasonably quickly. Different levels of handwriting are called for at different times. Writing for presentation or special occasions might require a careful, deliberate approach which is more time-consuming than a legible, day-to-day hand. There are also times when writing is personal to the writer and not to be read by others, so a lower standard of legibility is appropriate.

There are four important horizontal points:

ascender line
mid-line

baseline
descender line

Ascenders are the vertical strokes that rise above the mid-line on letters like 'd';

Descenders are the vertical strokes that hang below the baseline on letters like 'g'.

For adults only the baseline is visible; for children other lines have to be used carefully because there is a danger that they will measure the length of a stroke by the distance to the line and not by understanding the differences in letter size.

In order to understand words fully, your child has to write them as well as read them. But the motor skills needed to write letters are challenging because they are small, precise movements demanding an appropriate grip of the writing implement. There are things you can do to prepare your child for these movements:

✪ Let your child use large, water-based markers or felt-tips and large sheets of paper from time to time. It can help with letter formation because the pen grip is easier.

✪ Opportunities to use large paintbrushes on large sheets of paper are good, too.

✪ Most of the time, your child should be encouraged to create their own marks but, at other times, you can show them specific patterns and letter shapes for them to copy.

Christopher Jarman[3] suggested that the patterns shown in the illustration below can be a good way to practise forming letters appropriately.

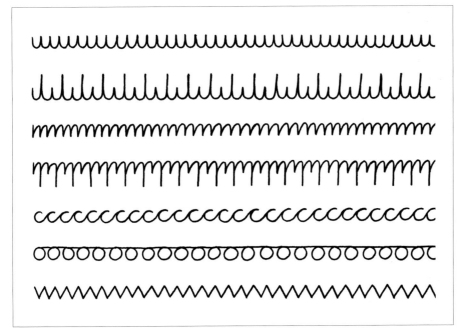

Christopher Jarman's pre-writing patterns

Forming letters

Once your child is ready to write their name using conventional English letters, they need to be taught how to form the letters accurately. Here's how you can help:

✪ Using unlined paper is good because it encourages your child to find a horizontal level in relation to the edge of the page.

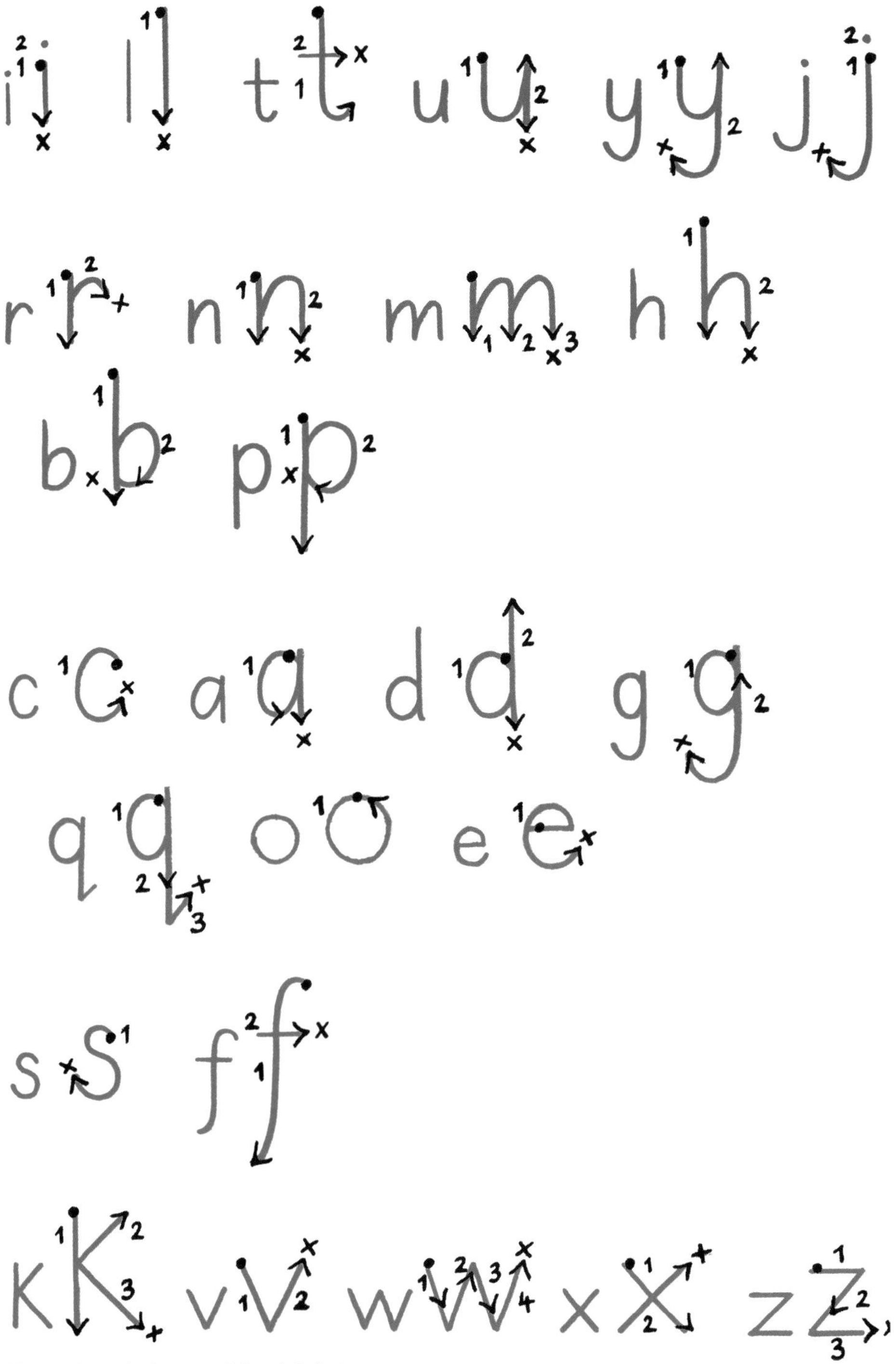

i j l t u y j

r n m h

b p

c a d g

q o e

s f

K v w x z

How to form the letters of the alphabet

✪ At other times, you can draw a horizontal line on a blank sheet of paper on which you can encourage your child to locate the letters of their name.

✪ Sometimes you can hold their hand to guide it. Don't worry too much about the size of the letters at this time. Large letters can be a good way to start learning the movements. In time, quite a lot later, children learn that they need to reduce the size of their writing to fit with the lines that are in their school books.

✪ Start with the first letter of the name, ensuring that it's a capital letter. Show your child how to write the letter and, while you do this, talk them through the strokes.

✪ Once your child can write the first letter of their name reasonably well, move on to the next one. Remember how important it is to help them to know the entry stroke of the letter.

To give an example of teaching the letters in a name, let's take the name Esther. I would begin:

'You start the capital E at the top, here, then do a straight line down. Then go back to the top and draw a line across, like this. Then go to the middle and do the same. The last line is at the bottom, like this. See if you can do it.' And carry on lin the same way.

If you want to help your child with the other letters of the alphabet, it's a good idea to teach letters in families that share similar pen strokes. The page opposite shows the letters in families and how you should help your child to form them. How to join the letters comes in the next chapter.

Why spelling's so tricky

You've seen that your child will engage in mark-making of all different kinds. Later, they learn to write their name and begin to understand about letters. But this seems a long way from the kind of conventional writing of words that we all know. Even when children have been taught how to form the letters of the alphabet, it doesn't mean they can write. To do this, they have to understand how to combine letters to make the meanings of words. This is spelling. And I wouldn't be surprised if there are a few words that even you still find tricky to spell — I know I do!

A brief history of English

Why is English spelling so tricky? It's mainly because it's not a one-hundred-per-cent phonetic language, like Spanish or Finnish; a significant minority of its words are phonetically irregular. George Bernard Shaw cleverly illustrated this. He asked,

Do you know what 'ghoti' means?
The answer is 'fish'.
If you take the sound of 'gh' in enough the 'o' in women and the 'ti' in station you get fish!

It is the irregularities of English spelling that make it demanding to learn. One of the main reasons why English spelling is phonetically irregular is because of the many influences on the language throughout history. During the fifth century, the Anglo-Saxons settled in England and, as always happens when people settle, they brought changes to the language, which was at that time 'Old English'. The texts that have survived from this period are in four main dialects: West Saxon, Kentish, Mercian and Northumbrian. The last two are sometimes grouped together and called Anglian. West Saxon became the standard dialect at the time but is not the direct ancestor of modern standard English, which is mainly derived from an Anglian dialect.[4] If you take the modern word 'cold' as an example, the Anglian 'cald' is a stronger influence than the West Saxon version, 'ceald'.

In the ninth century, the Vikings brought further changes to the language. Many place names were affected: 'by' meant a village, so Grimsby was Grim's village; 'thwaite' meant a clearing and 'mickle' was the Norse word for large, so Micklethwaite meant 'large clearing'.

The pronunciation of English speech was affected, too, and it's possible to recognize some Scandinavian-influenced words because of their phonological form – how they sound. One of the most interesting things about Scandinavian loanwords, as they are called, is that they are such commonly used words: sister, leg, neck, bag, cake, dirt, fellow, fog, knife, skill, skin, sky, window, flat, loose, call, drag, and even they and them.

In more recent times, words from a range of countries have been borrowed. Here's a small selection of examples:

French – élite, liaison, menu, plateau.
Spanish and Portuguese – alligator, chocolate, cannibal, embargo, potato.
Italian – concerto, balcony, casino, cartoon.
Indian – bangle, cot, juggernaut, loot, pyjamas, shampoo.
African languages – banjo, rumba, tote, zombie.

However, for many words it's difficult to attribute them to one original country. To illustrate the complexities of detecting where words originated, let's look at the word 'chess':

> *'Chess' was borrowed from Middle French in the fourteenth century. The French word was, in turn, borrowed from Arabic, which had earlier borrowed it from Persian 'shah' ('king'). Thus the etymology of the word reaches from Persian, through Arabic and Middle French, but its ultimate source (as far back as we can trace its history) is Persian. Similarly, the etymon of 'chess', that is, the word from which it has been derived, is immediately 'esches' and ultimately 'shah'. Loanwords have, as it were, a life of their own that cuts across the boundaries between languages.[5]*

The influence of loanwords is one of the factors that has resulted in some of the irregularities of English spelling. David Crystal[6] lists some of the other major factors. In the Anglo-Saxon period there were only 24 graphemes (letter symbols) to represent 40 phonemes (sounds). Later 'i' and 'j', 'u' and 'v' altered from being interchangeable to having distinct functions, and 'w' was added, but many sounds still had to be shown by combinations of letters.

After the Norman Conquest, French scribes – who were responsible for publishing texts – re-spelled a great deal of the English language. They introduced new conventions such as 'qu' for 'cw' (queen), 'gh' for 'h' (night), and 'c' before 'e' or 'i' in words such as 'circle' and 'cell' to replace 's'. Once printing became better established, this added further complications.

In the West, Johannes Gutenberg (1390s–1468) is credited with the development of movable metal type in association with a hand-operated printing press. William Caxton (1422–91) is often credited with the 'invention' of the printing press although other nationalities, such as the Chinese and Koreans, had used methods of printing centuries before.

Many of the early printers working in England were foreign (especially from Holland) and they used their own spelling conventions. Also, until the sixteenth century, line justification (lining up all the beginnings and ends of lines down a page) was achieved by changing the spelling of words rather than by adding spaces. Once printing became established, the written language did not keep pace with the considerable changes in the way words were spoken, resulting in weaker links between sound and symbol (that is, between speech and writing).

The importance of dictionaries

The publication of Samuel Johnson's dictionary in 1755 was a very important moment in relation to English spelling. Noah Webster, the first person to write a major account of American English (and whose name is still celebrated in the most important American dictionary: *Webster's*), compared Johnson's contribution to Isaac Newton's in mathematics. Johnson's dictionary was significant for a number of reasons. Unlike previous dictionaries that tended to concentrate on 'hard words', Johnson wanted a scholarly record of the whole language. His dictionary was based on words in use and introduced a literary dimension, drawing heavily on writers such as Dryden, Milton, Addison, Bacon, Pope and Shakespeare. Shakespeare's remarkable influence on the English language is not confined to the artistic significance of his work; many of the words and phrases of his plays are still commonly used today, as Bill Bryson[7] noted:

> *He coined some 2,000 words – an astonishing number – and gave us countless phrases. As a phrasemaker there has never been anyone to match him. Among his inventions: one fell swoop, in my mind's eye, more in sorrow than in anger, to be in a pickle, bag and baggage, vanish into thin air, budge an inch, play fast and loose, go down the primrose path, the milk of human kindness, remembrance of things past, the sound and fury, to thine own self be true, to be or not to be, cold comfort, to beggar all*

description, salad days, flesh and blood, foul play, tower of strength, to be cruel to be kind, and on and on and on and on. And on. He was so wildly prolific that he could put two in one sentence, as in Hamlet's observation: 'Though I am native here and to the manner born, it is custom more honoured in the breach than the observance.' He could even mix metaphors and get away with it, as when he wrote: 'Or to take arms against a sea of troubles.'

Johnson's work resulted in dictionaries becoming used as the basis for 'correct' usage for the first time. Dictionaries have a major role in the standardization of language and it's interesting to note that in modern times we have more than one 'correct' or standard English. For example, American English is represented by *Webster's* dictionary but English English is represented by the *Oxford English Dictionary* (although *Chambers* is the main source for word games and crosswords).

David Crystal[8] makes the point that although spelling is an area where there's more agreement about what is correct than in other areas of language, there's still considerable variation. Sidney Greenbaum's[9] research looked at all the words beginning with A in a medium-sized desk dictionary which were spelled in more than one way; he found 296. When extrapolating this to the dictionary as a whole, he estimated 5000 variants altogether, which is 5.6 per cent. If this were to be done with a dictionary as complete as the *Oxford English Dictionary*, it would mean many thousands of words where the spelling has not been definitively agreed. Crystal gives some examples including:

accessory/accessary; acclimatize/acclimatise; adrenalin/ adrenaline; aga/agha; ageing/aging; all right/alright.

Many of Greenbaum's words were pairs but there were some triplets, for example:

aerie/aery/eyrie

And there were even quadruplets:

anaesthetize/anaesthetise/anesthetize/anesthetise.

Names translated from a foreign language compound the problems, particularly for music students:

Tschaikovsky/Tchaikovsky/Tschaikofsky/Tchaikofsky/ Tshaikovski.

How children learn to spell

✪ One of the *most* helpful things that you can do is to encourage your child's experimentation with spelling – this is called *invented spelling*.

✪ One of the *least* helpful things that you can do is to insist on correct spelling before your child is ready.

✪ The balance is sometimes hard to get right, but it can be useful to know a little about the ways that children's spelling typically develops – find out about this below.

Richard Gentry[10] usefully identified five broad stages that represent children's spelling development. He identified these stages by analysing the writing of a boy called Paul Bissex whose mother wrote a book all about his reading and writing development. The title of Glenda Bissex's[11] book was taken from one of her son's early signs: GNYS AT WRK (genius at work). Since then other researchers have confirmed that the stages are a good representation of spelling development. You can see the five stages below, but I've only shown you examples of writing from the first two stages because they are the most relevant in this chapter. Examples of writing from other stages will feature in later chapters.

Stage 1: Mark-making and letter strings

This stage covers the child's earliest attempts at mark-making through to the stage when they use strings of letters, often not separated by word spaces. When you ask your child what the strings of letters mean they will tell you, but it's not normally possible to identify individual words. The letters of the child's name are often used more than others as they are the most familiar. The sample (right) shows this spelling stage.

An example of mark-making and letter strings

In the sample on page 122 the child has a clear idea of the meaning of the writing because the teacher has been able to scribe it underneath. The child has written strings of letters so there are no words or word spaces. Some letters are more common than others, such as A and M, so these might occur in the child's name. Some things you can do at this stage are:

✪ **Provide good resources for writing. Introduce special resources from time to time.**
✪ **Talk to your child about their drawings and writing. Suggest things they might draw or write next.**
✪ **Involve them in the writing that you are doing, such as writing a shopping list; writing their name and a message on greetings cards.**
✪ **Make books with them.**
✪ **Scribe their ideas using their words and phrases.**
✪ **Have somewhere to display their writing: magnets on the fridge; a pin board; in a clip frame, for example.**
✪ **Show them how to write their name.**
✪ **Show them how to form the letters of the alphabet.**

Stage 2: Semi-phonetic
The sample below shows a child's spelling at this stage.

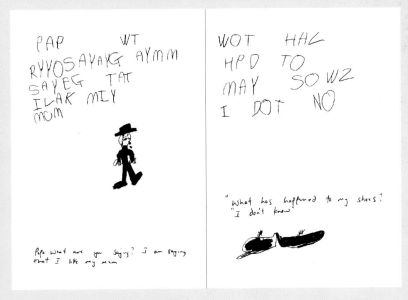

An example of semi-phonetic spelling

At the semi-phonetic stage, your child is becoming aware that there's a link between sounds and letters. They use the first letter of a word, particularly consonants, more confidently than vowels. The child knows the names of the letters and is aware that those letters can be linked to a variety of sounds. They understand what words and spaces are.

The extract on the previous page is taken from a little booklet that the child made. The pictures are particularly striking in this example. The wonderful thick black lines contrast with, for example, the detail of the tears of the boy who is crying and the laces on the shoes. Structurally, the child hasn't yet learned that the pages in a booklet should maintain some kind of continuous narrative; in this example they read like separate ideas. Once again, the teacher has written underneath the child's writing: 'Papa what are you saying? I am saying that I like my mum;' and 'What has happened to my shoes? I don't know.' You can clearly see that the child is confident with the more regular sounds of consonants. Notice also the use of a 'letter name strategy'. On the left-hand page, in the phrase 'what are you saying', the word 'are' is written as a letter R followed by a Y. The letter name R sounds just like the word 'are', so this is a logical idea and it's something that children at this stage often experiment with. The Y at the end may reflect the child's feeling that the word should have more letters in it, but doesn't remember which ones.

Things that you can do to help at this spelling stage include most of the ideas from the previous stage plus some new ones:

✪ **Stick labels on some objects in the house: door, fridge, cupboard.**
✪ **Talk about how to sound words out.**
✪ **Show them how to spell words then encourage them to Look, Cover, Write, Check. That means: Look at the word; Cover the word; Write the word from memory; Check if it's right.**
✪ **Play word games.**

Stage 3: Phonetic

Your child's invented spelling is full of words which look the way they are sounded out, like 'becos'. This is the point where they need to learn that English spelling has many visual patterns, for example words like: en**ough**; thr**ough**; **our**s; **y**ours. Your child also needs to develop their visual memory of whole words, syllables and other word chunks.

Stage 4: Transitional

Conventional spellings are frequently being used. Invented spelling is characterized by fewer phonetic strategies and more visual ones. The number of letters and choice of letters in difficult words are mainly right.

Stage 5: Conventional

The majority of words are spelled in a conventional way. Your child is becoming aware of the fact that writing can be carried out in more than one draft. In the first draft the transcription aspects, such as spelling, can be left to be proof-read at a later stage. Your child is aware of things like computer spell-checks and dictionaries. Your child will make very close guesses about unfamiliar words, such as technical vocabulary.

That knotty problem: punctuation

Your child has learned that writing communicates meaning in a different way from pictures. They have learned that meaning is contained in words. At this stage your child will not have much understanding about punctuation, but it's useful if you are aware of some basic principles so you're ready to help. Over time, your child needs to understand that spoken language is not organized in quite the same way as written language. Written language is organized in sentences, whereas speech is organized in units of information.

How would you answer this question, 'What's a sentence?' I'll go into the grammar of sentences in the next chapter but, for now, it's useful to have a definition. The simplest and most accurate description of a sentence for children is that it's something which makes complete sense on its own and *usually* begins with a capital letter and ends with a full stop. This is *not* a sentence: 'Apple the ice green' because it doesn't make sense! This *is* a sentence: 'World War Two bomber found on Moon' — this bizarre headline appeared in a tabloid newspaper a while ago! Newspaper headlines and advertisement texts often lack a full stop but they still count as sentences.

Nigel Hall[12] has done some useful research on children's punctuation. Incidentally, he was the person who gave Lynn Truss the joke which formed the title of her book *Eats, Shoots and Leaves.*

A panda walks into a restaurant, sits down, and orders a sandwich. He eats the sandwich, pulls out a gun, and shoots the waiter dead. As the panda leaves, the manager shouts, 'Stop! Where are you going? You shot my waiter!'

'I'm a PANDA!' the panda shouts back. 'Look it up!'

The manager opens his dictionary and reads:

Panda *A rare mammal akin to a bear with black and white markings native to a few mountainous areas of forest in China and Tibet. Eats, shoots and leaves.*

Hall suggests that there are two main aspects of children's understanding of punctuation: *graphic punctuation* and *linguistic punctuation*. From about three years old onwards, if you draw your child's attention to punctuation marks as part of their reading, they may experiment with the marks in their writing, in what appears to be a random fashion. A good example of this is the child who puts a full stop at the end of every line on a page rather than at the end of each sentence. Your child is playing with the marks. This is what Hall means by graphic punctuation.

Later, they realize that you can't just put punctuation marks anywhere. Gradually, children's knowledge and understanding of punctuation increases and they learn that the purpose of punctuation is to enhance meaning and avoid ambiguity. This requires linguistic understanding. Here's a nice piece of punctuation ambiguity. It appeared as a moving banner caption at the bottom of the screen on *Sky News* at the time of the floods in New Orleans (I'm grateful to Helen Hancock, editor of the *Primary English Magazine*, for sending me the example).

Bush: One of the worst disasters to hit the US

The use of quotation marks (' ') would have helped to avoid the suggestion about his competence as President!

Here are some things to do to help your child's understanding move from graphic punctuation to the linguistic punctuation of later stages:

✪ **Discuss punctuation marks you see in print at home and outside.**
✪ **Say the name of the punctuation marks as you read aloud.**

✪ Use punctuation when you scribe for your child. When writing a caption, use two sentences so that there's a need for punctuation.

✪ Play games where your child has to do a particular action and/or sound instead of each punctuation mark in the text. (Comedian Victor Borge used to do a funny routine like this which you can listen to on the internet at geocities.com/Vienna/1864/b-mus-1.htm).

✪ Make sure you are clear about what punctuation marks do. Pauses to breathe are only one relatively minor part of their use.

In later chapters, I'll cover how the different punctuation marks are used.

Expectations for a child's writing at age four

What you can expect	What you can do to help
Understands distinction between print and pictures.	Talk about the differences between pictures and print. Show what you do when you write and tell your child that you are writing.
Plays at writing.	Provide a range of accessible resources. Encourage the use of writing as part of role play.
Assigns meaning to own mark-making.	Ask your child about their writing and discuss its meaning with them. Set them challenges to write things for you, such as little notes.
Often chooses to write names and lists.	Help your child to write their name properly. Encourage them to sign their name on greetings cards.
Uses invented spelling.	Encourage your child to have a go at writing and spelling in their own way. Once they have the confidence, help them move towards conventional spellings.
Has knowledge of letter shapes, particularly those in own name.	Teach your child how to form the letters properly. Teach them how to write their name.
Recognizes some punctuation marks.	Help them to recognize the difference between letters and punctuation marks.
Knows about direction and orientation of print.	Talk to your child about left and right, top and bottom. Use your finger to point as you read from time to time. Ask questions to encourage your child to show you their knowledge about orientation of print.

age four
to seven

Wonderful books

In the last chapter I showed you the first book that we made with Esther as a way of illustrating how you can scribe for your child's writing. Olly's first book didn't happen until he was 5y 4m, which was considerably older than Esther. He didn't show the same interest in bookmaking, although he was interested in writing in general when he was younger. At the time I'd been thinking about how I might tap into his interests in order to engage him in some writing. He was very interested in the latest craze for Digimon and Pokemon (short for Pocket Monster) cards. Knowing that many boys are interested in non-fiction texts, I suggested to Olly that we work on an information book about Digimon. He wasn't sure how to go about this so I showed him how we could plan the book on paper first. I folded two sheets of A4 paper into quarters so that each quarter could represent one page of the finished book. On the right you can see one of these planning pages and the pages of the finished book are shown opposite.

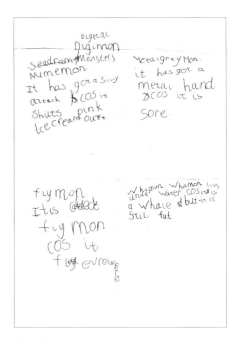

Olly's Digimon planning page

We caught part of the process of writing the first draft on video. Here's an extract, with my comments alongside:

Conversation	My comments
OLLY: [How do you] spell ice-cream?	As usual I want to start by emphasising the amazing capacity that children have for learning. You can see the hard thinking that is going into the spelling. The discussions that we had with him about letter names and phonemes when he was younger are now
DAD: I, C, E.	
OLLY: I, ... C.	
DAD: That's right.	
OLLY: E. E /k/. That /k/?	
DAD: C, yeah.	
OLLY: /k/ /r/ /reem/ – What's after	

Page 1: Whamon. Whamon lives under water because it is a whale, but it is still fat...POP!

Page 2: Venommyotisimon. Venommyotisimon has got big hands and big legs and has got holes in its wings... WHOOSH!

Page 3: Numemon. It has got a silly attack because it shoots pink ice cream out...YUM YUM!

Page 4: Togemon. Togemon is a spiky plant with boxing gloves on...OWW!

Page 5: Metalgreymon. It has got a metal hand because it is sore...OWW!

Page 6: Flymon. It is called Flymon because it flies everywhere...ZOOM!

Page 7: Lillymon. Lillymon shoots a screw out for an attack... CRACK.

Cover

Olly's Digimon book pages

Conversation

/r/. Dad, what's after /r/?

DAD: What's after what?

Olly: What's af...

DAD: Um, C, R, E, A, M.

OLLY: E,...A. ...Ice-cream...Pink ice-cream.

DAD: Yeah, OK. Right then, what's next?

OLLY: Um...[*looking at sheet of Digimon characters*] not sure I know about them.

DAD: You know more than I do... Do you know anything about that one [one of the Digmons]? ...

OLLY: I'm just going to, writing about what it's got on it.

DAD: OK ...

OLLY: It...on the top...could just put a line there. It. It, it, has [*Olly is speaking the words as he writes them*]...has got, got, got a. They all. These two [i.e. the sentences] are both starting with 'it has got a'. A metal, metal.../taul/ metal, hand when /h/ /a/ /n/. /han/ /d/... hand and, and, hand and, little hand...hand.../be/ /cos/ it is sore! [*laughs*]

DAD: Yeah, it's good.

OLLY: It's a bit, it's not real but...

DAD: That's all right, you can make it up can't you? Just gives you ideas.

My comments

beginning to pay off. The way that writing phonemes supports learning to read phonemes is apparent. When Olly is trying to spell ice-cream I say the letter C. When he comes to write 'cream' he checks that C is the same as the phoneme /k/ – a very good example of the way that the phoneme is different depending on the word in question: soft C for 'ice' and hard C for 'cream'.

There are some good examples of Olly's ability to reflect on his written language use (showing his metalinguistic awareness). He notices that two of his sentences start with the same phrase: 'It has got a...' He also comments on the fact that the word /sau/ can reflect two different meanings, 'saw' and 'sore' although he mixes the two up (see end of conversation).

Olly realizes that what he is writing is 'not real'. This is an important issue for non-fiction writing; the extent to which the information is accurate or not. On this occasion

Conversation

DAD: **Um.**

OLLY: **Sore.**

DAD: **S.**

OLLY: **I want you to spell.**

DAD: **O,...R,...E.**

OLLY: **Sore. That's the sore that you saw something.**

DAD: **No that's, um, S, A, W.**

My comments

the purpose of the activity was to encourage him to write so I didn't want to insist on particular kinds of information. In fact, the text was a mix of fiction and non-fiction.

I also want to point out the thought processes that were going on in my mind to help his learning. First of all, I encouraged the task originally because making a book is a good thing to do. On this occasion I gave him the spellings because I wanted him to keep his composition going. Also he was at the phonetic stage in his spelling (see the section *Going beyond sounding words out* on page 149) so he was ready for more emphasis on conventional spellings. However, remember that there's always the potential problem that children's composition can grind to a halt if they are continually asking for correct spellings. I also helped Olly with the overall structure of the writing, from the beginning of the process and throughout. I suggested when he should finish one page and move to a new page so that he didn't get stuck. I acknowledged that he knew more about the subject than I did (which was true) with a view to building his confidence. And at the end of the extract I corrected his misconception and gave him some information about the different meanings of 'saw' and 'sore'.

So, to summarize the help you can give to a child who's not so eager to write:

✪ **Try to find a subject and format they're really interested in.**
✪ **Help with suggestions about structure and content so your child doesn't get stuck.**
✪ **You may sometimes want to give help with spellings to keep the composition flowing.**

Another example of a wonderful text is one of Esther's pieces of writing. At the time, she was approaching her Key Stage 1 (age five to seven) statutory tests and had been encouraged to write a story of her choice. The writing was then sent home along with instructions for homework. When we first saw the piece we were overjoyed to read what was a wonderful story. The homework required us to help correct any transcription errors. It was clear that Esther was not keen on further redrafting because she felt it was finished. I suggested that we might work together on the computer, but this made no difference. In the end, I typed up the piece in the hope that some comparison might be made between my transcription and hers. But she remained adamant that the piece was finished. You can see the original handwritten piece opposite.

There were numerous things which I felt were lively and held my interest. The opening beckons the reader into the story:

> *Well come her[e] and I will tell you a story,*

This was possibly influenced by a picture book called *The Dancing Frog*, by Quentin Blake which we had at home. There were various aspects which represented typical features of narrative, such as the use of dialogue, the moral to the story and the further explicit messages to the reader:

> *and you can guess what happened.*

Examples such as:

> *good litel girl;*
> *where having brecfast;*
> *very bad FIRE!*

in particular, the use of capitals and an exclamation mark illustrate the description and detail.

The writing had a cathartic element represented by the coming to terms with one of life's many rites of passage: losing a tooth. All writers generate ideas by explicitly and/or implicitly reflecting on their own life. It contained a mystery to challenge the mind of the reader: could it be that only orange teeth would put out a fire? The best texts leave unresolved questions and food for thought. It gave personal messages to the reader, playfully disrupting fixed ideas about textual forms.

THE TOOTH FIRE

One day a little girl lost 1 of her teeth. Her name was Cloe. Cloe was a good litel girl. Her tooth looked orenge.

The next day Cloe and her mummy Where having brecfest When the paper came. I will get it! Said Cloe. Mummy mummy! IN the paper it Said there is a very bad FIRE! Well come her and I will tell you a Story When I was a little girl and there Was a FiRe. And I had Just Lost a tooth and it was Orenge. And I Said to my Mum can I thro my tooth away Wy donht you tho it in the FiRe. So I Said OK. And can you ges wut hapend the Fire Whent out. Shal I do that...iF you Wish. So She Whent to Find the Fire. She thro the tooth into the fire and it aventiouce it Went out. EVrewon cneard and Shouied. WEL DONE CLOE. Then Cloe run home and toled her mummy. Mummy I put the FiRe out. Wel done nowe you no Wat to do with yor tooth.

Esther's story

The influence of other texts (*intertextuality*) is represented on a number of levels: the asides to the reader, the very bad fire in the newspaper, the potential influence of *The Dancing Frog*. The writing also mirrored some of the emotions to do with self-confidence which were a feature of Esther's life. Narrative has always been a vehicle for exploring emotions.

But the most extraordinary revelation came only after I had discussed the process of writing. Esther was sitting next to her friend Gill at school. She had just written the title for the piece. Gill said, 'That's not how you spell "fairy", that says "fire".' Rather than correct the spelling, Esther constructed the complete narrative on the ideas of a tooth and a fire; like a metaphysical conceit perhaps! The creative dexterity and cognitive challenge of this is fascinating but, overall, it reinforced my belief that when we think about children's writing we must take account of the process, not just the end product.

When will my child write words?

I'm going to start this section with a look at Olly's development of writing words. Before I do, here's what I think was his first joke. At two-and-a-half he saw a daddy-long-legs and said to me, 'That's you!' One of Esther's first jokes was to say to Olly, 'I'm not a bib, you know!' when he inadvertently dribbled on her. Ah, the wonders of children's humour! But, seriously, both jokes show an increased knowledge and awareness of words.

When he was 2y 0m we recorded in the diary that Olly was sitting at the table using some felt pens. After a while he said, 'I can't do a D, you do a D,' and handed me a pen. I drew two Ds and he made a mark as if copying. Then he said, 'Do a /d/, mummy.' At 2y 1m he said, 'I going to do my name,' then he drew a circle and said, '/o/, /li/.' In the same month there was an example where Olly spent quite a while using wax crayons. He kept saying things like, 'I done a /o/,' or 'That's a /d/.' At one point he suddenly shrieked, 'McDonalds!' When I looked at his paper he'd made a mark that looked like a letter M. When he was 2y 6m I was working at the computer with him. He said he wanted to write 'mummy's name'. I spelled out the word 'mummy' by saying the names of the letters. When I said U, Olly said, 'That's not me!', joking about the fact that the letter name sounded like the word 'you'. At this point in his development he thought that words were written with one letter. At 2y 7m Olly found a pen in our bedroom and said, 'I want to write right now!' On another occasion when Olly was 2y 9m, Esther and Olly worked together on finding small pictures inside a big picture in a Noddy magazine. Esther had been asking me about writing the names of the pictures. When she went to get dressed Olly, who had been learning from my explanation to Esther, decided to try writing his own letter shapes.

In Chapter 1, I explained the importance of your child's name as one of the first words that they learn to read.

✪ **It helps your child's reading and writing when you show them how to write their name.**

On another occasion in the same month Olly decided he wanted to do some writing. When his mum came into the room he had independently written 'Oller' with the bottom part of the letter E reversed. Later in that month his mum was writing a shopping list and Olly asked for a paper and

pen so he could write one as well. His mum told him what she was writing and asked him what phoneme each word began with. He knew nearly all of the initial phonemes of the words. He then tried to write the first letter of each word.

When Olly was 3y 5m old, the kids were writing Christmas cards. When we gave him the letter names he was able to write his friends' names on their cards. In the same month Olly was watching a video of Cinderella. Independently, he decided to do some writing. He wrote, 'Cinderella, prince, dress'. Apart from the writing of names, this was the first time that he'd independently written something with his own intended message.

At 3y 8m he was reading a book called *Big Bad Pig*. He asked about the meaning of the phrase 'This Walker book belongs to...' which was printed on the inside cover. The following morning he got up, came downstairs and wrote, 'Esther and Olly and Mum and Dad' in very neat black handwriting in the inside cover of the book. That same morning, as I was writing the diary entry about the event and looking at Olly's writing, he added an exclamation mark. Then he added some commas after most words, saying that his teacher had used them.

We recorded Olly's first invented spelling at home at 4y 8m. I'd suggested that he might like to draw something from *Thunderbirds*. Olly wrote 'Thunderbird 2' with the letters 'SGOT'. As you saw in Chapter 4, his '1, 2, 3, 4, 5, Once I caught a fish alive' writing when he was 4y 9m was a more extended example of the use of invented spelling. At the same age he also wrote his first piece of extended independent writing with his own intended meaning, as opposed to being derived from a text that he already knew. He spent at least 20 minutes working on the piece. The audience for the writing was members of the family, although he decided in the end it was a song and was written for Esther because she had earache.

Esther's first independent writing of a word other than her name was recorded at 4y 1m. Her first piece of extended invented spelling, at 4y 10m, was:

Esther and Olly rsitigon thecher onthe sdaj
(Esther and Olly are sitting on the chair on the stage).

Another lovely example of invented spelling came the following month:

> *hte e sd dune is cumitow giv sum esdreds to t cids*
> (The Easter bunny is coming to give some Easter eggs to the kids).

It's difficult to pinpoint exact moments when reading and writing begin because there are so many aspects of learning that contribute to, and are indicative of, that development. However, in the table below I've attempted to summarize my children's ages when key things happened in terms of their writing, and have compared these with similarly significant moments for reading.

Key moments in the development of writing and reading

	Esther's age	Olly's age
Writing: first independent writing of name	Unknown	3y 1m
Writing: first invented spelling of a word other than child's name	4y 1m	4y 8m
Writing: first extended writing of child's own composition using invented spelling	**4y 10m**	**4y 9m**
Reading: first sounding out of a word	3y 8m	3y 1m
Reading: first decoding of the sentences of an unknown text	**4y 6m**	**4y 4m**

Esther was always more keen to compose writing, including invented spelling, than Olly, so her first invented spelling of a word other than her name happened considerably earlier. The bold entries in the table are more typical of the overall comparison of their reading and writing development. At the time of writing, the differences shown have proved to predict similar slight differences in attainment in formal tests at school.

In answer to the question I posed as the heading for this section, I think that if you put into practice my advice in this book, your child should be able to write their first pieces of several sentences (although not necessarily punctuated) of their own composition, using invented spellings, between the ages of four and five, although this would represent an early start. I'd expect children in general to do this between the ages of five and six. Children who don't write like this by the age of seven are a cause for concern but, as I said in Chapter 2, this is not something that should engender high levels of anxiety. They are likely to need more intensive support in school, based on a full understanding of the many factors that can be responsible for children not learning to write early.

You shouldn't say it like that! Grammar

Most people think that to learn 'correct' grammar you simply have to understand the rules and obey them. If you believe this, then it follows that all you have to do is teach your child the rules and correct them if they break the rules. But if you think like that, you won't help your child as much as you could.

✪ **You need a well-informed understanding of a few key principles of modern grammar to help you help your child. Find out more in this section.**

Language works according to four key principles:
1   The communication of meaning is the driving force.
2   All language users seek to avoid ambiguity.
3   Language is governed by conventions (rather than rigid rules), some of which change over time.
4   New forms of language evolve in order to find more efficient and quicker ways to communicate meaning.

This book has emphasized throughout how important point one is. This chapter concerns itself with point three in particular. Grammar is one of the most important parts of language. It's the way that words and sentences are put together in order to express meaning. It's also one of those subjects, like apostrophes, neat handwriting, the Queen's English, and so on, that can get some people quite worked up! Here's a brief example.

My mother and father had come to visit one weekend and I was talking to them about the children. In the course of the conversation I said, 'The kids were sat watching the TV.' Here's a rough idea of how the conversation continued:

MY MUM: **Sitting.**
DOMINIC: **What?**
MY MUM: **It should be sitting. The kids were sitting watching the TV.**
DOMINIC: **No, it shouldn't.**
MY MUM: **Yes, it should.**
DOMINIC: **How do you know?**
MY MUM: **I just do.**
DOMINIC: **'Sat watching' has become standard English.**
MY MUM: **No. It's just wrong.**

Now, I fully accept that I could have been wrong (although I didn't accept this at the time of the argument of course!) because the point about whether 'sat watching' has become standard is rather difficult to prove, but I stick by the general principle which was at stake. At the heart of all these kinds of arguments are different views about how language works. Some people believe that there's a fixed set of grammatical rules which you simply have to learn in order to speak and write correctly. People with this view can be called *prescriptive* grammarians. Most modern linguists take a different view. They see language as something to be described and analysed in order to understand the way that it is used. They are *descriptive* grammarians, and they are interested in the way that all language-use reflects a particular context, such as the social background of the speaker and the setting in which the message is communicated. This kind of information needs to be taken into account when analysing language and suggesting the rules that are at work. The idea that particular features of language are correct or incorrect is simply a product of someone's judgement, not an absolute rule.

Claims about incorrect language-use typically focus on a tiny proportion of the language. In other words, more than 99 per cent of our speech doesn't cause anyone to claim that it's incorrect, but there are a few phrases which repeatedly cause disagreement. The argument with my mother was based on a disagreement about one phrase. I suggested that although 'sitting watching' may have been the convention in the past, 'sat watching' was increasingly being used. The fact that language changes over time is a very important part of understanding grammar. If you accept this, it can be illogical to argue that some phrases are definitely right or wrong. But, just in case you think I'm suggesting that anything goes, the following is definitely incorrect: 'rules are grammar no there for.'

Spoken v. written language

It's important to make a distinction between the ways that you help children with their spoken language versus their written language. Spoken language is more closely related to the identity of the speaker than written language. You can see this in the way that people get more irritated when someone tries to correct their speech than if they do the same with a draft of writing. All feedback, whether about spoken language or written language, requires sensitivity, but this is particularly the case with spoken language. It's also important to recognize that some unconventional spoken grammar is a product of your child's language development which will correct itself through day-to-day conversation, whereas other patterns, particularly as children get older, may benefit from your more direct input.

Esther has tended to use unconventional grammar in her speech slightly more than Olly. Here are some examples:

A big tree what drooped over.
Is there any onions left?
There probably isn't any [tortilla wraps for a sandwich].
What I bought [referring to something that she had bought].

My attempts to correct these kinds of examples started to meet with resistance. Esther quite reasonably argued that it was her language so she could speak how she wanted to. I was certainly not prepared to prejudice my relationship with her over something that was likely to right itself given time. A tack that sometimes worked when she was older (about ten onwards) was if I said, 'I'll shut up if you can tell me what the standard English should be.'

Children are capable of subtly switching their language according to the context they find themselves in. So, if they have to talk politely to their friends' parents, their language will be more formal than when they are chatting to their friends. Remember Harry Enfield in his Kevin sketches?

Good teaching at school encourages the use of drama to explore situations that require different levels of formality in language use. Within a drama context, the teacher can suggest conventional forms of language to pupils, who find the advice less personal because they are in role. Focusing on the conventions of written language is similarly less personal, but can still have a positive effect on spoken grammar. The conventions for writing are also more firmly standardized than for spoken language so more correction is required.

More about defining a sentence

Your child has learned that writing carries meaning. They've learned that this meaning is contained in words which are made up of letters. One of the important things they have to learn next is that writing is constructed in sentences. The control of sentences is a vital part of good writing. As I showed in the section on the difference between speech and writing (see Chapter 1, page 41), the sentence is a unit of written more than spoken language. In the last chapter I defined what a sentence is, but the explanation was incomplete, something which I want to come back to here.

Your child will have experimented with a range of punctuation in a graphical way, but the first punctuation they need to understand linguistically (that is, in its proper grammatical use) is the full stop. We often say that a full stop is used to mark the end of a sentence, but this begs the question 'What is a sentence?' People also often say that a sentence is something that begins with a capital letter and ends with a full stop. This is a bit of a circular description: 'a full stop is used at the end of a sentence and a sentence has a full stop at the end'! It's also a linguistically limited explanation. Sentences sometimes end with question marks or exclamation marks. Many printed sentences lack punctuation, such as newspaper headlines. Spoken sentences do not have a perceptible capital letter and a full stop either.

There now follows a brief but, I hope, not too painful grammar lesson! I give you this information not because you need to teach it to your child, but because, armed with this knowledge, you will be better informed and therefore more likely to be able to help your child's writing.

The following explanation is based on David Crystal's[1] work. The diagram on the next page gives an overview of the different ideas that I'm going to cover.

Minor sentences such as, 'Hello', 'Eh?', 'Like father, like son', 'Wish you were here' and 'Taxi!' are irregular (Ronald Carter[2] argues that these might better be called *utterances* because they do not contain a *clause* – see below).

Major sentences are what we usually mean when we refer to sentences. There are two types of major sentence: a *simple sentence* or a *multiple sentence*.

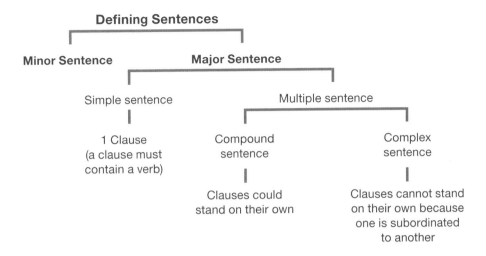

Defining Sentences

A simple sentence contains one *clause*. A clause must contain a verb and is built from *clause elements* (which consist of one or more words).

Clause element	Subject	Verb	Object
Clause (also a simple sentence in this example)	You	threw	a stone.

A multiple sentence contains more than one clause. There are two main types of multiple sentence:

1 A *compound* sentence: the clauses, which could in principle stand as sentences on their own, are linked by coordinators, such as 'and' or 'but'.

Example: 'I like his hat [*main clause*] but I don't like his coat [*main clause*].'

2 A *complex* sentence: the clauses are linked by *subordination* with words like 'because', 'when', 'although'. One clause (the subordinate clause) is subordinated to another (the main clause). The subordinate clause cannot stand as a sentence on its own because it relies grammatically on another clause. The information it contains is in the background compared to the main clause.

Example: 'I answered the door [*main clause*] when Jane rang the bell [*subordinate clause*].'

For those of you who are grammatically challenged, I remind you of the actor Martin Jarvis's witty comment that a subordinate clause is one of Santa's little helpers! (Another of Lynn Truss's[3] gems). So, according to David Crystal a sentence is:

✪ a construction which can be used on its own, without people feeling that it is incomplete;

✪ the largest construction to which the rules of grammar apply (descriptive rules rather than prescriptive rules);

✪ constructed according to a system of rules which are naturally acquired by nearly all the mother-tongue speakers of the language. A sentence formed in this way is said to be grammatical.

All of which is a slightly lengthy explanation of why a sentence is not only something that begins with a capital letter and ends with a full stop! However, I reiterate the point that the simplest and most accurate description of a sentence for children is that it is something that makes complete sense on its own and usually begins with a capital letter and ends with a full stop.

Now, before I dive into correcting sentences, here are some of the things you can do to respond to children's writing and encourage the use of grammar and punctuation.

✪ **One of the best ways you can help your child to write in sentences is by working with them throughout the time of writing; and/or by interacting with them at a point during the process; and/or talking about the writing once they have finished.**

✪ **Say something specific about what you liked in the writing. A general comment such as, 'That's lovely!' is good, but a more specific comment such as, 'Wow, I love the way that the girl danced!' is even better.**

✪ **Often you don't need to comment on the unconventional features of the writing, such as lack of capital letters and full stops, because you don't want to dampen your child's motivation for writing. But there will be occasions when you do want to focus directly on the transcription elements.**

✪ **A good question to ask which encourages children to think about their writing is, 'Do you know where the full stops should go?' This prompts them to think for themselves. If they really don't know, you can always say, 'Shall I show you?' and then simply add them to the** writing. If it's a very short piece, it might be a good idea to write it out on another sheet of paper for comparison. This avoids defacing your child's writing.

It's easy to see from these suggestions the way that grammar and punctuation are closely linked. Having prepared the ground with the short lesson on grammar, let's turn to some specifics of punctuation.

Punctuation

A common characteristic of children who are learning how to punctuate sentences is the use of 'and' as a proxy for a full stop. The writing on the right is a lovely example.

    First of all, can you work out the meaning of the piece? Here's a bit of help: the 'Hojibs' are a tribe that Neil invented. If you're still struggling with the words, try reading the writing out loud in a Cockney accent (a really clear example of the way that spoken language influences children's written language). Neil's writing is full of imagination, particularly

One day to romens was going to a nother Land and the to romens got Cart in a tarat and the PiePol was the hoJibs and the romens was very sade and one of the romens had a arrow went in his haed the romen was buring the other romen.

Neil's writing

the way that he used his knowledge of the Romans in conjunction with the Hojibs. As far as his sentences are concerned, in nearly all cases he can replace the word 'and' with a full stop and capital letter. Conventional punctuation for the piece might be like this:

> *One day two Romans were going to another land but they got caught in a turret by the Hojibs. One Roman was very sad because the other had been shot through the head by an arrow. The Roman who lived had to bury the one who had died.*

By the end of the four-to-seven stage in their development, children should have learned to punctuate their sentences with capital letters and full stops. Other punctuation marks that are learned at this stage are different end-of-sentence ones, such as the exclamation mark and the question mark. One of the most useful marks, and one of the easiest to misuse, is the comma. Here's my definition:

> **Comma** *Separates clauses and clause elements in a sentence in order to clarify meaning and to avoid ambiguity. Has many other uses but particularly to separate items in a list or items in sentences which have list-like structures. Indicates a slight pause in the flow of the sentence.*

The key phrase in this definition is 'to clarify meaning and to avoid ambiguity'. There's an old-fashioned idea that every clause in a sentence should be separated by a comma. This is simply not true. Frequently people use too many commas. At other times, sentences can have more than one possible meaning because a comma hasn't been used to avoid ambiguity. Even the queen of punctuation, Lynne Truss, fell into the trap of insisting on one too many commas. The title of her book *Eats Shoots and Leaves* is, of course, based on a potential ambiguity. The insertion of a comma could turn the title into one suitable for a scene in *The Godfather*. But look at an example that she gives in the book. Truss says that one of the uses of the comma is to help

> *when two complete sentences are joined together, using such conjunctions as and, or, but, while, and yet.*

The example she gives is:

> *The boys wanted to stay up until midnight, but they grew tired and fell asleep.*

There's absolutely no need for the comma. It would make no difference to the meaning if it was removed. Therefore the only justification for including the comma is because Lynn Truss's rule says so. Truss has fallen into the trap of being prescriptive about language.

The advice that I gave for helping with capital letters and full stops also applies to commas. At the appropriate moment during the writing you should help your child to understand how the addition or deletion of a comma can help them to communicate their message more clearly.

Going beyond sounding words out

Here are two lovely examples of children's spelling attempts. Can you work them out?

My Klone

ches and unen

The first is a famous footballer from Liverpool. The second is a flavour of crisps.

In the last chapter we looked at what you could do when your child was at the mark-making, then semi-phonetic spelling stages. In this chapter we turn to the phonetic spelling stage.

Stage 3: Phonetic

Your child's invented spelling is full of words which look the way they are sounded out, like 'becos'. This is the point where they need to learn that English spelling has many visual patterns, for example words like: en**ough**; thr**ough**; **our**s; **your**s. Your child also needs to develop their visual memory of whole words, syllables and other word chunks. Neil's writing in the sample on page 147 is a perfect example of the phonetic spelling stage. The extract was part of a 12-page book that he wrote. He had a clear audience in mind, shown by the dedication he wrote to his mum and dad. Here are some things that you can do to help at this stage.

✪ **Provide good resources for writing. Introduce special resources from time to time.**

✪ **Talk to your child about their drawings and writing. Suggest things they might draw or write next.**

✪ **Involve them in the writing that you are doing, such as writing a shopping list; writing their name and a message on greetings cards.**

● Make books with them.

● Have somewhere to display and store the most interesting examples of their writing or pieces that they particularly like.

● Help them to see words in chunks: cup-board; h*ere*, th*ere*, everywh*ere*.

● Talk about print in the environment that is different from conventional forms, for example, Toys Я Us.

● Enjoy playing with language, for example tongue twisters and jokes.

● Play word games such as Hangman, simple crosswords, simple word searches, finding words within words (for example, there's an *ear* in my h*ear*t).

● Encourage learning words by analogy: f-ight; l-ight; n-ight; t-ight.

Joining letters: upper and lower case

During this stage your child can be taught how to write with joined-up letters. Joined-up writing is important because it's a key aid to fluent writing. An important principle about joined-up writing is that not all letters join. In the last century there were times when copperplate handwriting, which required all letters to be joined, was used. And England is not the only country to have tried this; France used to have a national handwriting style. The main problem is that when pupils have to write at speed this kind of joining completely breaks down because the movements are particularly inefficient. You need to lift the pen from time to time, in other words to break the join, in order to keep the hand moving fluently along the line.

Just as the letters of the alphabet were taught in 'families', the same is true of teaching the joins. The easiest joins, and the ones that may happen spontaneously, are those that join at the base line: i l t u h n m a c d e. The table on the page opposite shows the six families of letters for joining and those that don't need to join.

● It's a good idea to use writing your child's name as an example. Show them how to write their name with joined-up writing, remembering that the capital letter is one of those that doesn't join.

The families of joins[4]

iluhnmacek	These letters join spontaneously at the baseline.
ft	'f' joins from the crossbar; 't' can also join this way.
orvw	These letters all join from the top.
acdgoq	The join to these letters goes over the top and back.
gjyq	The first three letters can be left unjoined or loop from the descender. 'q's join is unique.
pb xz s	'p' and 'b' can join or not as you please. 'x' and 'z' are probably better not joined, and 's' joins more efficiently when simplified.

When joins are taught in this logical way children can easily see how they work. Already there are possibilities for discussion on such matters as whether to join certain letters ('r' is one that is sometimes better left unjoined) and whether some letters need modifying before they can join efficiently.

Is copying the same as writing?

One of the issues to do with teaching children to write is the role of copying. Copying is useful when learning the appropriate letter formation and joining for handwriting but, overall, when children copy they are only learning a limited range of skills. They may be learning something about forming the letters although, if they are copying from a computer font, this learning is minimal because the letters are not formed in the same way as handwritten letters. Your child may also be learning something about the way that words are spelled when they copy, but their concentration is more likely to be on each letter rather than learning words as a whole. The act of copying might help their reading a little if they are reading the words as they copy them. Certainly, children should be encouraged to read as they copy because this stops them losing their place. You could say that copying is rather similar to decoding without meaning when reading. If writing involves the composing of meaning, then copying is not really writing.

Olly, more than Esther, spontaneously copied text from his picture books. On a few occasions he got quite excited about seeing how many pages of writing he could do.

✪ There's no harm in copying, but it shouldn't be the dominant method to help your child learn to write.

✪ You need to encourage your child to see writing as a way to compose meaning first and foremost.

Expectations for a child's writing at age seven

What you can expect	What you can do to help
Occasional interest in copying known texts.	Encourage this provided it does not become the main form of writing over time. Use the opportunity to help with letter formation and whole-word memory.
Range of genres of chosen writing more limited, reflecting specific interests and motivation.	Encourage your child to follow the things that they are interested in and to write about those topics.
Able to write longer texts, such as stories.	Children's stamina for writing improves as the conventions of handwriting and spelling get a little easier. They will still need help with structuring their texts as they try to control these longer forms.
Understands the need to make changes to writing.	Help your child to see how redrafting writing can help them to get better outcomes.
Understands that writing is constructed in sentences.	The understanding of what a sentence is, and its punctuation, should be getting stronger.
Word segmentation secure and all phonemes represented in invented spellings.	Help your child by engaging them with the visual aspects of words. Word games, word chunks, etc. should be the focus to help them understand English spelling.
Use of punctuation for meaning. Full stops used conventionally.	Help your child to organize their writing in sentences and to remember to check for capital letters and full stops.
Handwritten print of lower- and upper-case letter-shapes secure.	Keep an eye on letter formation and remind your child from time to time if they are not forming letters conventionally.

age seven to eleven

Wonderful writing

Children at this stage do more and more writing at school and, even at the primary phase, they are set writing tasks for homework. A consequence of this is that spontaneous writing of longer forms at home becomes rarer. Some children do continue with diaries, scrapbooks and albums, poetry and stories, but more often it's the day-to-day fragments of writing such as lists, tables, charts and so on which become the norm. If the educational system encouraged more sustained writing, based on children's choices, then more might be continued at home but the highly prescribed regime of writing different genres and writing exercises continues to run the risk of demotivating children.

In the month before his tenth birthday Olly wrote at school a modern version of a fairy tale which you can see below. It was aimed at Year 6 (ages ten to 11) and Year 7 (ages 11 to 12) readers.

I've argued that one of the important things to consider is how you should respond to your child's writing in a way that is most likely to help them improve further. At this stage it becomes increasingly difficult to make quick responses. The sheer amount of words that children can

---

Little Dead Riding Hood

Once upon a time, there was a little girl called Little Dead Riding Hood. She lived in a forest somewhere over there. One day her mum asked her to take some atomic cakes to her granny's house. Little Dead Riding Hood got in her Aston Martin DBS and drove slowly to granny's. Suddenly a Keonigsegg CCX skidded to a halt in front of Little Dead Riding Hood. "Where do you think you're going?" asked the wolf.

"I'm going to my granny's, to give her these atomic cakes," replied Little Dead Riding Hood.

"Cool" said the wolf, as he threw a sleeping gas bomb into the Aston Martin.

"I... feeeeel... sleepy"

The wolf drove to granny at 285mph. Hang on Keonigsegg CCX don't go that speed. OK he went at 250mph. Is that better? Yes, that's better. When he arrived at Granny's he ate her up but found out that the clothes didn't fit, so he got back into his car and drove to Tesco. When he had found some clothes he teleported back leaving his Keonigsegg CCX in the car park. With the keys in he got into Granny's bed and Little Dead Riding Hood came in.

"Grandma what big nose you have!" said Little Dead Riding Hood.

"All the better to eat you with," replied the wolf as he lunged towards Little Dead Riding Hood. Little Dead Riding Hood pulled out 2 ak47s and blasted the wolf to bits.

"Teacher you to not lunge at people pretending to eat them," said Little Dead Riding Hood. At that instant an army tank bashed through the wall, firing at will. In about half a second the house had fallen on Little Dead Riding Hood

---

compose, particularly in stories, means you have to take considerable time to read the piece. As I was preparing this section I read through Olly's story in full twice. I then made some notes about the things I liked and the things that I thought could be improved. This took me about 30 minutes which means that you'll need to put aside the same amount of time to respond effectively to your child's writing in the latter years of this stage.

Things I liked in Olly's story included the witty title, Little Dead Riding Hood, which fits well with the untypical fairy tale ending:

> *So, amazingly, for once in a fairy tale they didn't live happily ever after.*

I was attracted to the deliberately casual language of:

> *She lived in a forest somewhere over there.*

Olly's use of modern imagery clashes with what we expect in a fairy tale, for example his continuing interest in cars is used to good effect. Also the effect of the 'atomic' cakes is imaginatively portrayed:

> *...I...feeeeel...sleepy.*

The narrator's aside was cleverly done:

> *The wolf drove to granny's at 285 mph. Hang on Koenigsegg CCXs don't go that speed. OK he went at 250 mph. Is that better? Yes, that's better.*

(I learned that a 'Koenigsegg CCX' is a car!) The writing style reminded me of *The Stinky Cheese Man and*

and as you could probably guess, she died. So amazingly, for once in a fairy tale they didn't live happily ever after.

A very clever ending to your story and some excellent complex sentences. Well done (HP)

Olly's story: 'Little Dead Riding Hood'

Other Fairly Stupid Tales which is a brilliant book by Jon Scieszka and Lane Smith.

To improve the writing I'd suggest that he needed to resolve some things that are unclear. For example, why did Little Dead Riding Hood drive 'slowly' to Grandma's in her Aston Martin DBS? It was also not clear why the wolf left his car in the car park at Tesco and was suddenly able to use a teleporter. Olly's response to this was that the story was full of things that weren't meant to make sense. In fact, he said that none of it was meant to make sense so he felt that these were consistent. However, there is a difference between random nonsense and nonsense that is cleverly structured for comic effect, which it seems to me he achieved most of the time. At first I wasn't sure whether the fact that Grandma had a big nose which was all the better to 'eat' Little Dead Riding Hood with was deliberate. Before I asked him about this, Olly spontaneously volunteered how much he liked that bit because it was deliberately silly. The final point I'd make is that I'm not in favour of gratuitous violence in children's stories, but nor do I think it should be censored all the time. In this case I think that the violence fits well with the style of humour and the use of modern knowledge in a traditional genre, although some of you may find it a bit much.

You'll notice that my suggestions for improvement have focused entirely on the composition, not on the transcription elements. Proof-reading needs to be done *after* other aspects, such as structural ones, have been redrafted. As it happens, there are few problems with spelling, punctuation and grammar but these could be dealt with reasonably quickly by encouraging him to proof-read at the end and, if necessary, helping him to identify the errors.

The teacher's comment was, 'A very clever ending to your story and some excellent complex sentences. Well done. House point.' Generally, his teacher's feedback was helpful but, as for all teachers, it was driven by government agendas. The statutory tests require the use of complex sentences (see Chapter 5, page 145, for the explanation of a complex sentence) to achieve the highest marks, so teachers dutifully drum this into their pupils' heads. You'll have seen that the teacher ticked the word 'lunged', presumably because it represents a verb that isn't used very often by children at this stage, but didn't comment on the humour of a big nose to eat you with.

Helpful feedback

Here's an example of another child's writing and the kind of feedback that can be given. He was a child I taught many years ago. As part of the teaching week I used to have a morning called 'writing workshop'. This gave children opportunities to carry out writing of their choice and to 'publish' the ones they liked for peers and other people to read. James had spent two terms during the weekly writing workshop on his story called 'The Grass Gods'. The final draft was some 20 pages of A4 arranged in 12 short chapters:

1   End of school
2   The scrap piece of paper
3   The White Fleshed Emperor
4   Where do they start?
5   Giant Corner
6   The Dark Forest
7   Died of fright!
8   The Poisoned Sword
9   Magic is in the air
10 The cave
11 Peter does something good!
12 Home Sweet Home, but not for long!

The story began like this:

> *'Class dismissed,' said the class teacher after school.*
> *'Hey Thomas,' said Peter to his best friend Thomas,*
> *'Thanks for helping me with my maths and for all your set-ups to seal my hat-trick.'*
> *Thomas asked him if he wanted to come to sleep ...*

Although I'd normally try to respond orally to drafts of writing during the workshop, on this occasion I took the book home and prepared a written response. James was then encouraged to respond in writing to my points. You can see my comments and James's responses on the next page.

The Grass Gods

My written comments

Do you need the first part of chapter two? Could the end of chapter one ('maybe he could be that brave...') go straight to page three 'NEVER, NEVER, NEVER'?

James's written replies

Yes I think that is a good idea but I would have to change the name of chapter 2 (The scrap piece of paper).

Page 3
Should this be like this? Thomas you have destroyed our land...<u>said the strange voice</u>.

Yes I think the spooky voice is good.

Page 6
Where do they get the key from? Do you think this is clear in the story?

No I don't think this is very clear. But they get it on the roof of the door. My new sentence would be... It's on the narrow stone on the top of the door.

Page 7
I don't understand 'It's on the top of the roof!'

This means the boy.

Page 8
First the White Fleshed Emperor helps them then he threatens them. Do you want him to be a friend or an enemy?

This White Fleshed Emperor is a friend but he wants them to do the mission. He would be cross if they did not do the mission because they were the ones who started the adventure in the first place.

Page 9
Your pictures of the giants are excellent. It works well as you turn the page.

Story structure

Longer texts, like the examples you have just seen, require children to have new understandings of structure and form. Sometimes further work on these longer texts may be set for homework. At school your child will learn about the ways that different texts are structured so it's useful if you have some understanding of this.

One of the most commonly cited ideas about the organization of texts is related to story structure: the idea that stories have a beginning, middle and end (or as Philip Larkin mischievously suggested a beginning, muddle and end). In Australia a group of academics who became known as the genre theorists[1] developed the simple idea of beginning, middle and end to suggest that narratives had a six-part structure:

Abstract; Orientation; Complication; Evaluation; Resolution and Coda.

David Wray and Jane Medwell[2] simplified the technical language and related the structure to *Little Red Riding Hood* in order to illustrate this structure. You can see the result below.

The six stages of a narrative

Martin *et al.*	Wray and Medwell	
Abstract	Title of the story and introductory ideas	*Little Red Riding Hood*
Orientation	Setting of the story including characters	A forest and the two cottages
Complication	The main event	Red Riding Hood meets the wolf dressed as her grandmother
Evaluation	The impact of the main event on the characters	She runs away and finds the woodcutter
Resolution	The final implications of the main event	The woodcutter kills the wolf
Coda	Ending the story	The moral

Structures like this are one way to think about the extent to which the writing is coherent. Each stage requires the one before it if the text is to make sense. Of course, one of the interesting things about any kind of model like this is the way that so many texts do not simply conform. Traditional tales like *Little Red Riding Hood* are often used as illustrations to show how such structures work. However, narrative is a wildly diverse form which resists simple classification. How well would this structure apply to some of the following: the script of the film *Pulp Fiction* which contains three linked stories; multi-author internet texts; 'Choose your own adventure' books where the reader can make choices as to how the plot will unfold; or *Bridget Jones' Diary*? You'll also be familiar with narrative devices such as flashbacks (for example, *Carrie's War*, by Nina Bawden) and traditional stories told from different points of view (*The True Story of the Three Little Pigs:* Scieszka and Smith, 1989) which challenge the idea of simple linear structures.

Although control of the overall structure is important to writers, for the intelligent reader it's only one way, and arguably a superficial one, of analysing texts. For example, you might choose to analyse the story of *Little Red Riding Hood* by exploring the idea that it is overtly about the dangers of child abuse. This might seem a bit extreme or to be reading too much into the text (how can one read too much?). However, a useful website[3] provides a translation of Perrault's original written version:

> *The wolfe seeing her come in, said to her, hiding himself under the clothes. Put the custard, and the little pot of butter upon the stool, and come into bed with me. The little red Riding-Hood undressed her self, and went to bed, where she was very much astonished to see how her grandmother looked in her night-cloaths...*
> *THE MORAL...*
> *With luring tongues, and language wondrous sweet,*
> *Follow young ladies as they walk the street,*
> *Ev'n to their very houses and bedside,*
> *And though their true designs they artful hide,*
> *Yet ah! these simp'ring Wolves, who does not see*
> *Most dang'rous of all Wolves in fact to be?*

The line of analysis we've chosen to take here has a historical angle, introduced by locating one of the original written versions of the tale (although, like other traditional stories, these started their lives as oral tales). The analysis also has a social dimension by suggesting a link with abuse. The 'moral' of the tale, written in rhyming couplets, once again leads to the question of whether the narrative structure illustrated above can universally be applied.

The idea that forms of writing can be reduced to simple structural models is common and applies to other texts too. For example, there are several books on the market which suggest how a Hollywood screenplay should be structured. The debate continues as to how useful they are.

The examples of writing used so far in this chapter are fiction, but one of the changes to primary education over the last ten years has been the emphasis on a wider range of other text types in schools.

Different kinds of texts

We all have to be able to write a range of text types in day-to-day life, so the argument goes that children need to be taught these, too. However, how many text types do you use regularly? Lists, notes, greetings cards, emails, letters, perhaps?

Texts for work vary dramatically according to the type of work, and tend to fall within quite restricted and increasingly specialized types. These are usually best learned about in the context of the workplace, often through collaboration with colleagues, and are refined through awareness of the readers' responses. In fact, that's a pretty good model for learning writing generally.

Six non-fiction text types have been identified in genre theory: recount, report, procedure, explanation, persuasive argument and discussion. Find out more about what these titles mean in the table on page 164.

Writing frames

The research from the 'Exeter Extended Literacy Project' (EXEL) developed the idea of *writing frames* as a way of supporting children's non-fiction writing. David Wray and Maureen Lewis[4] explain the notion of writing frames and how they can help in the following way:

Writing frames are outline structures, enabling children to produce non-fiction writing in the different generic forms. Given these structures or skeleton outlines of starters, connectives and sentence modifiers, children can concentrate on communicating what they want to say. As they practise building their writing around the frames, they become increasingly familiar with the generic forms.

One of the important ideas behind writing frames is that they are intended to support writing done in meaningful contexts, where appropriate audiences and purposes have been identified.

The *argument* genre has proved one of the most demanding for both teachers and children. The example below shows how a child used a writing frame: the child's text is in italic; the frame text is in normal type.

Although not everybody would agree, I want to argue that
Children should not wear school uniform.
I have several reasons for arguing for this point of view.
My first reason is
That they feel more comfortable in clothes which they choose to wear. They would feel more relaxed and be able to work better and concentrate more on their work.

Non-fiction genre forms

Genre form	Example of text
Recount	Witness statement
Report	The Rose Report on the teaching of reading
Procedure	Recipe
Explanation	Instructions for model
Persuasive argument	Text putting forward a point of view, such as 'smoking should be banned'
Discussion	A government Green Paper

Another reason is
> *There wouldn't be the problem of parents not*
> *wanting to buy uniforms because they think they are too*
> *expensive.*

Furthermore
> *Sometimes you might wake up and find your two lots*
> *of uniform in the wash.*

Therefore, although some people argue that
> *Children might take it past the limits.*

I think I have shown that
> *Children should be able to choose their clothing just*
> *as adults do, as long as they wear sensible clothes.*[5]

The writing frames are designed to be applied flexibly and it is intended that children should move towards writing without the use of frames. One of the potential problems is the over-use of frames, which can restrict writers because they feel constrained by the language of the prompts.

Although there are some benefits to the consideration of genre structures, there have been certain problems. Once again, the most fundamental has been the classification of the six non-fiction genres. How does it help children to be taught what a 'procedure' genre is when they could more usefully refer to and discuss different recipes and recipe books, for example, or other examples of real texts that contain procedures? Another problem is that teachers frequently rely on published schemes which have examples of texts created by the consultants to the scheme. These examples may well reflect the writers' genre theory description, but they have little resemblance to real texts.

One aspect of the *procedure* genre has been the idea that these texts use imperative language to adopt an impersonal tone. The examples usually used are recipes. But the assumption doesn't hold up when you analyse real recipe books. Frequently, books include authors' reflections about the food that they are enthusing about. Here's Madhur Jaffrey:[6]

> *This simple chicken dish is a great favourite with our*
> *children. I generally serve it with plain long-grain rice*
> *and 'Whole green lentils with garlic and onion'.*

Hugh Fearnley-Whittingstall's *The River Cottage Meat Book* includes his 'meat manifesto' which argues passionately for the importance of high-quality, preferably organic, meat. Even in the instructions for recipes, the texts are made more interesting by personalising the commentary, as Gary Rhodes[7] does:

> *Add the eggs and blitz for a further 1 minute. Add the cream, brandy and jus, if using. (The jus is optional for this recipe, but I find it gives a little depth and flavour to the parfait.)*

In spite of these examples, it's true that recipes do use imperative language, clearly shown by the verb regularly appearing at the beginning of the sentence, as in 'Add the eggs...' But this feature is a very insignificant one and there are better ways to learn about how to write recipes.

✪ **The best way to learn about a genre is to read texts in that genre. For example, the best way to learn about writing recipes is to start by making and eating food with your child, moving on to a personal collection of favourite recipes laid out in a way that is of interest to the writer and likely readers, just like best-selling cookery books.**

Subheadings and paragraphs

In addition to the features of specific genres of writing, the overall structure of a piece of writing is also revealed by the following things:

- ✪ the amount of words;
- ✪ the title;
- ✪ chapters – if the text is suitably long;
- ✪ subheadings and sections;
- ✪ paragraphs;
- ✪ general layout features.

The amount of words for a text is one important feature of the structure. It's possible to write about a topic in 100 words, 1000 words, 10,000 words or 100,000 words. A piece of 100,000 words is book length and requires chapters. A piece of 100 words is abstract length and may or may not require paragraphs. An interesting aspect is the title; it's often written last, whereas children are usually encouraged to write the title first.

Subheadings are used to divide the text into large sections. Like the title, the subheading should clearly sum up the content of the section. Too few subheadings can make it more difficult for the writer to communicate the flow of the argument if writing an essay, for example. Only very skilful writers can maintain clarity in long pieces without subheadings (stories are different from other kinds of writing since the narrative maintains the flow). However, too many subheadings can break the flow of the writing, which can distract the reader from the intended meaning.

One of the things that your child will learn about towards the end of this stage is how to structure writing in paragraphs. A paragraph is a block of text which consists of a number of sentences about a particular topic. The first sentence of a paragraph is often referred to as the 'topic sentence' because it reveals to the reader what the paragraph is about. It's very rare to have a paragraph of only one sentence – your child should be taught to spot these and check to see if the sentence would be better joined to the paragraph before or after. The paragraphs in a subheaded section represent a sequence of ideas that the writer puts forward. They must have a logical order to them. The last sentence of one paragraph leads the reader into the topic sentence of the next paragraph. However, this flow of ideas is subtle. It's not that an explicit link needs to be made between paragraphs. It's more that the careful placement of paragraphs and use of sentences will result in the logical order and satisfactory flow of ideas.

More on punctuation

A punctuation riddle: What do *Ulysses*, *Angela's Ashes* and the Ginn Reading Scheme have in common? Answer: they all have punctuation missing. I apologise for reducing James Joyce's masterpiece *Ulysses* to a discussion about punctuation (just a tiny part of how he challenges conventions). However, the last 36 pages of the book are unpunctuated apart from an asterisk at the beginning and a full stop at the end (although the very end features punctuation of a much more physical kind which brings the book to a memorable climax). Here's a sample:

> *Yes because he never did a thing like that before as ask to get his breakfast in bed with a couple of eggs since the City Arms Hotel when he used to be pretending to be laid up with a sick voice doing his highness to make himself interesting for that old faggot Mrs Riordan that he thought he had a great leg of and she never left us a farthing all for masses for herself and her soul greatest miser ever was actually afraid to lay out 4d for her methylated spirit telling me all her ailments she had too much old chant in her about politics and earthquakes and the end of the world*[8]

Frank McCourt manages perfectly well without a single speech mark
throughout *Angela's Ashes*:

> *Philomena said, There is a suspicion you might have*
> *Presbyterians in your family, which would explain what*
> *you did to our cousin.*
>
> *Jimmy said, Ah, now, ah, now. 'Tisn't his fault if*
> *there's Presbyterians in his family.*
>
> *Delia said, You shuddup.*
>
> *Tommy had to join in. What you did to that poor*
> *unfortunate girl is a disgrace to the Irish race and you*
> *should be ashamed of yourself.*
>
> *Och, I am, said Malachy. I am.*
>
> *Nobody asked you to talk, said Philomena. You done*
> *enough damage with your blather, so shut your yap.*[9]

The early stages of the Ginn Reading Scheme also neglect speech marks,
but for reasons which are unclear.

> *Stop it.*
> *It is not here.*
> *It is not in my home.*
> *I can help you look.*[10]

Which brings me to one of my hobby-horses. Why are children taught to use
double marks to punctuate speech when most children's books use single
marks? This is a typical example of where custom and practice continue
without analysis of conventions that are actually in use. Good teaching,
at home and at school, requires the analysis of relevant, high-quality *real*
texts as the basis for showing examples of the conventions of language.

The remaining punctuation marks

To be quite honest, these marks are ones that tax adults, let alone
children, but they are ones that are covered by the end of primary school,
so here's a reminder of how they are used:

Semicolon (;)

Separates main clauses that are not joined by a coordinator which the semicolon replaces (a coordinator is a word which links parts of a sentence. The most common coordinators are 'and', 'or' and 'but'. Some people call these conjunctions). The two parts of the sentence (the main clauses) are equally important. Represents a break in the flow of the sentence which is stronger than a comma but weaker than a full stop.

Example: The people in the first group were hard-working; those in the second were lazy.

Colon (:)

Separates a first clause, which could stand as a sentence, from a final phrase or clause that extends or illustrates the first clause. If in doubt don't use a colon mid-sentence, use a comma instead. Most commonly used to introduce things like lists or examples.

Example: I went to the shop to buy the following: an orange, two pears and a packet of crisps.

Apostrophe (')

This is the punctuation mark that probably catches more people out than any other. There are four main uses:

1 Contraction: didn't = did not.
2 Possession singular: the cat's tail, the child's book.
3 Possession plural: the cats' tails, the children's books (as 'children' is an irregular plural word in itself, the apostrophe comes before the 's').
4 Possession with name ending in 's': Donald Graves' or Donald Graves's book.

Common errors include:

This first happened in the 60's. (60s is now the convention.)

Was that it's name? Confusion of its (possessive) and it's (contraction, as in: It's [it is] my party and I'll cry if I want to). This possessive form is irregular and does not have an apostrophe (Was that its name? is the correct form).

Despite my reservations about some of Lynn Truss's theories about punctuation in *Eats, Shoots and Leaves*, I couldn't help but join her in apostrophe-error spotting. I saw this in an advert in the *Yellow Pages*:

Success comes in cans...
...failure comes in cant's
For literature, web sites and multi-media
with real design fizz call the people that can.

A positive interpretation of this advert is that the error in 'cant's' is a clever deliberate mistake which reflects what will happen if you don't get your design done by this company. If it *isn't* deliberate, then discerning customers should go elsewhere for their design needs!

Parenthesis (can be indicated with dashes or commas but most effective with brackets, such as the ones surrounding this comment).
Structurally-independent words or phrases which elaborate the meaning of the sentence and which can be separated by brackets.

Hyphen (-)
Links words or phrases to clarify meaning.
Example: We must re-form the group (clarifies that this is not the word 'reform').
Indicates that words are part of a single expression.
Example: The children were involved in role-play.

Dash (–) or (—)
The length of the line is given different names. One name is the en-dash (–) which is used, for example, to indicate a page range: pp23–35. The em-dash (—) is longer and can be used to mark parenthesis (but see above). It can also be used to indicate part of a sentence added as an afterthought, but I'd recommend that a comma is often better for this. In reality we usually use the hyphen key on the keyboard for most of these because it's easier than using the insert menu's 'insert symbol', 'special characters' function.

Slash (/)
Often used to indicate words or phrases that are used interchangeably.
Example: The statutory tests/'SATs' were carried out on the same day.

Ellipsis (...)

Indicates where something has been omitted. Often used to show that part of the text from a quote has been omitted. Also used in fiction writing to indicate an unfinished thought or to imply continuation of thinking.

Example: John said, 'I wonder if I could...' but then he was rudely interrupted.

Quotation marks (" ") or (' ')

Many fiction books show direct speech punctuated with single marks whereas others use double marks.

Other uses of quotation marks include double marks to indicate a quote from a published source.

Example: Wyse said that "the teaching of formal grammar does not help children to write better".

Single marks can be used to show that an expression is in everyday use but is not academically precise.

Example: The children take their 'SATs', which technically should be 'statutory tests' because SATs are a brand in America.

Single marks can also be used to indicate that you are referring to a word or letter rather than using it as a normal part of the sentence.

Example: The word 'cat' begins with the letter 'c'.

To conclude, here are some further ideas for developing your child's understanding of punctuation. In a useful article by David Waugh,[11] he suggests using comic strips and speech bubbles and converting them into text-only to help children understand how to punctuate speech. Waugh also suggests 'walking and reading' where the reader has to stop walking at a punctuation mark. Discussion about how meaning changes according to the way punctuation is used is prompted by the following example:

PRIVATE. NO SWIMMING ALLOWED.
PRIVATE? NO! SWIMMING ALLOWED.

Here are some more suggestions for things you can do to help with grammar and punctuation:

✪ Collect examples of unusual punctuation from adverts, signs, game cards and so on.
✪ Use mobile phone texting and internet conventions to see the imaginative ways that different marks are used.
✪ Encourage your child to notice punctuation in the texts that they see around them. Analyse real texts, looking for the different ways that punctuation is used.
✪ Use the shapes of the marks as the basis for design and pattern work.
✪ Personify punctuation in drawings and as characters: the aggressive exclamation mark; the laid-back back slash; the no-nonsense full stop.
✪ To bring the marks alive use sounds and/or actions to highlight their presence. The comedian Victor Borge did this famously (have a listen at http://www.geocities.com/Vienna/1864/b-mus-1.htm). Other ways include saying the name of the marks when reading aloud to highlight their presence and doing different actions to accompany the different marks. To extend the focus on sound, musical instruments could be used to create different sounds associated with different marks in a text.
✪ Concentrate, overall, on motivating children with writing activities and supporting them to use the most appropriate punctuation for the messages they wish to compose. This is more useful than teaching punctuation through decontextualized tasks.

The final spelling stages

Just before I cover the final two spelling stages, here are a couple of examples of the way that modern forms are adding to spelling. Try to work this text out:

FeudTween 2hses- Montague&Capulet. RomeoMfalls_ <3w/_JulietC@mary Secretly Bt R kils J's Coz & is banishd. J fakes Death. As Part of Plan2b-w/R Bt_leter Bt It Nvr Reachs Him. Evry1confuzd-bothLuvrs kil Emselves

Surely the shortest version of a Shakespeare play ever! The idea was developed by student mobile service 'dot.mobile'. There are now extensive internet dictionaries covering the different signs and symbols used to communicate through mobile phones and email. Here's a very small selection from *Netlingo*.

@>--;--	A rose
:-x	Kiss
:-*	Kiss on the cheek

And how about *Star Wars* the feature film in ASCII characters? Try asciimation.co.nz/. All of these should be enthusiastically discussed with your child because they offer the chance to reflect on how they differ from conventional forms of spelling. This kind of discussion helps your child understand conventional forms stimulated by interesting examples that are different from the norm.

The final two spelling stages that you would expect your child to pass through are described below.

Stage 4: Transitional

Conventional spellings are frequently being used. Invented spelling is characterized by fewer phonetic strategies and more visual strategies. The number of letters and the selection of letters in difficult words are mainly accurate.

The child whose writing is featured in Sample 1 on the page opposite spelled many words using standard spelling. He was using visual patterns but sometimes selected the wrong pattern, for example 'outher' instead of 'other' ('out' and 'her', perhaps); 'dore' instead of 'door'; 'notest' instead of 'noticed'. He was encouraged to think about methods to remember the correct patterns and to commit the words to memory using 'Look, Cover, Write, Check' (see page 178).

Stage 5: Conventional

The majority of words are spelled in a conventional way. Your child is becoming aware of the fact that writing can be carried out in more than one draft. In the first draft the transcription aspects like spelling can be left to be proof-read at a later stage. Your child is aware of things

In less than ten seckond

Chapter 3 the hide a way

They got took back to the mans secret Hid out Where there
wos five other people who look ranthd nasty people. They put
Chris and Sophey in a cage and locked the done. They walk away to there
Table a few meters away from the cage they Sat down and sloder to
thakk. Then Shopey had a plan the notiest a Handel in the cage so they
puled the Handel a arrr r r r r r r r r r r r r r r r r r r r r
r r Ed!

They handed in a bed of money
cried
omoney chrid Chris
Said Sophy ?
Are you Shrove it is sacked Said Chris
"I Shrove I am sure Said sophey
"whats that over there said Chris
It wos a hote in the wall
" Shand we shouldt we. yes we will Chris said
"OK" sophy said
So they went thag the Hore hole and looched around.

Vent

I Happens

Sample 1: Transitional spelling

"How can you prove that your
not lying? asked mum. "Well
replied Molly, when I finished
brushing my teeth I went in-to
our bedroom to get changed. Polly
was in the bedroom. I said to
Polly why do you have to be so
naughty? Polly said she didnt now.
So I said to her well i'll tell
you a story because what you are
doing is wrong.

'ਤੇਰੇ ਕੋਲ ਕੀ ਸਬੂਤ ਹੈ ਕੀ ਤੂ ਝੂਠ ਨਹੀਂ
ਹੁਸਾਝੀ?" ਮੰਮੀ ਜੀ ਨੇ ਪੁੱਕਿਆ, ਮੋਲੀ ਬੋਲੀ,
"ਜਾਦੇ ਮੈ ਆਪਾਣੇ ਦੰਦ ਸਾਫ ਕਰ ਹਾਦੇ ਸੀ
ਇਹ ਮੈ ਕਪੜੇ ਪਾਉਣੇ ਨੂ ਅਸਾਦੇ ਕਮਰੇ ਚਲੇ ਗਾਈ
ਸੀ, ਪੋਲੀ ਕਮਰੇ ਵਿਚ ਸੀ, ਮੈ ਪੋਲੀ ਨੂੰ ਕਿਹਾ, ਤੂ
ਸ਼ਰਾਰਤ ਕਿਊ ਹੈ, ਪੋਲੀ ਕਹੀਂ ਮੈਨੂ ਪਤਾ ਨਹੀਂ,
ਇਹ ਮੈ ਉਸ ਨੂ ਕਿਹਾ ਕੀ ਮੈ ਤੈਨੂ ਇਕ ਕਹਾਣੀ
P.T.O

Sample 2: Conventional spelling

like computer spell-checks and
dictionaries. Your child will
make very close guesses about
unfamiliar words, such as technical
vocabulary.

It was suggested to the
child whose writing is shown in
Sample 2 on the left that she might
like to try a dual language text.
Having completed the first draft
in English, she took it home and
asked her mother to help her with
the written Punjabi. As well as a
number of minor errors, the child
substitutes 'now' for 'know'. This
is a common problem for more

experienced spellers. The word that was used is spelled correctly but is the wrong word for the context.

Things that you can do to help at these two stages are:

✪ Provide good resources for writing. Introduce special resources from time to time.
✪ Talk to your child about their drawings and writing. Encourage the development of writing preferences.
✪ Engage with their homework, including the learning of spellings.
✪ Help them reword information from various sources, such as the internet, so they understand it better.
✪ Help your child improve their proof-reading skills, including use of the computer spell-check.

✪ Have somewhere to display and store the most interesting examples of their writing or pieces that they particularly like.

✪ Help them to see words in chunks: cup-board; *here, there,* every*where.*

✪ Enjoy playing with language, for example tongue twisters and jokes.

✪ Play word games such as Hangman, simple crosswords, simple word searches, finding words within words (there's an *ear* in my h*ear*t).

✪ Show your child how dictionaries work. Find reasons to look words up with them.

✪ Encourage the use of learning words by analogy: f-ight; l-ight; n-ight; t-ight.

Once your child is mainly using standard spellings they will still need strategies to help them learn and remember problem words and new words. The computer spell-check can be a helpful tool but it must be used in the right way. The first difficulty that children need to understand is that if a word is spelled correctly, but is grammatically wrong, the spell-check will not detect it. Grammar-check may do, but I don't find the grammar-check as effective as the spell-check.

Each time your child uses the spell-check (or proof-reads their writing) they are given a reminder about particular words that they spell wrongly. In order to learn how to remember these words they need to think actively. The table at the bottom of the next page shows a framework for thinking about problem words.

Firstly, they need to identify which letter(s) in the word they find difficult to remember. Next, they must try to think of a logical way of breaking the word into smaller parts. It can be helpful to think about *stems*, *prefixes* and *suffixes*.

A prefix consists of a letter or letters placed at the front of a word or stem to form a new word.

Example: 'before' (**be**-fore); 'be' is the prefix and 'fore' is the stem.

A suffix consists of a letter or letters placed at the end of a word or stem to form a new word.

Example: 'shorten' (short-**en**); 'short' is the stem and 'en' is the suffix.

Finally, your child needs to try to use analogies with other similar words to help them remember the word next time. The key thing is that they share visual characteristics more than aural characteristics. In other words, they look similar rather than sound similar.

You also need to help your child to develop a range of other strategies to help them remember problem words. Here are some suggestions:

✪ Spelling 'rules'

Although there are always exceptions to spelling rules, the process of thinking about them and investigating the extent to which they work can help to improve spelling. One of the best-known rules is:
I before E except after C when the sound is /ee/:
Examples: field (ie), but receive (ei).

Another rule is that for words ending with a single consonant, preceded by a short vowel sound, you should double the consonant before adding the suffix:
Example: split – splitting; bet – betted.

✪ Developing the visual memory

Margaret Peters argued that spelling was largely a visual memory skill, so she encouraged teachers to use the strategy of 'Look, Cover, Write, Check'. This involves looking at the correct spelling of a problem word, covering it, attempting to write it, then checking to see if you wrote it correctly.

✪ Mnemonics and other devices

Think of 'necessary' as 'two ships on the sea' or 'two sleeves and one collar' (two Ss and one C).

A spelling strategy for problem words

Word	Difficult part	Breakdown
1 there	er	t + here
2 heard	ea	h + ear + d
3 tomorrow	m rr	to + morrow

✪ Sound out words as they look
/bus/ /ee/ /ness/ for 'business'

✪ Use a dictionary
A good dictionary, such as *Chambers* or *Longman's*, is a fascinating resource. Look up your problem words and read about their different meanings, and the different grammatical functions that they have. Greater knowledge about words and seeing them in the context of the dictionary can help jog your memory when you next come to write them.

✪ Play word games
Games like Scrabble, Boggle, Double Quick, Lexicon, crosswords, word searches, and so on, all require standard spelling. One of the interesting aspects of Scrabble is the way that very good players know all of the more than one hundred two-letter words there are. As part of your knowledge of word structures, it can be interesting to look at the way you can build on two- and three-letter words to construct other words.

As you've seen from the three chapters on writing in this book, there are many, many ways to help with spelling. So why is it that the most common approach to spelling is the word list sent home each week, followed by the dreaded spelling test on a Friday? There are many more active ways of learning spellings, as I've shown, than simply memorising lists. These could easily be set for homework. Even the task of parents helping their child to proof-read a piece of writing would be much more valuable than the repetitive weekly task of list learning. There's nothing wrong with trying to learn words but, like many things if done to excess, it becomes boring, which is not conducive to high levels of learning.

Similar words

1 here	the	where	then
2 heart	hear	earn	earned
3 tomato	tomography	borrow	follow

Oliver Wyse

The orange is nice because it is sweet whereas bananas aren't. Furthermore marmalade is orange. Although if it is made with lime it is made are green, nevertheless. Additionally bogies some people like to eat them. Afterwards their mouths stink. When you eat garlic. Eventually. Similarly I have used all the words!

Well done Olly

Olly's paragraph of spellings

One of Olly's responses to the weekly spelling homework task revealed much about his skill with language. You can see above that he was asked to put the list of spellings into a paragraph. In moderation, this is a good exercise because it requires understanding of the meaning of the words, not just rote learning. However, I can't help but wonder if the imagination used in this task could have been better used for a real piece of writing.

Testing, testing

The writing tests present a much more complex picture than the reading tests. Once again I refer to the 2006 test pack for my description. Although the specific tasks change each year, the basic principles are likely to remain the same (unless we manage to get the testing abolished in favour of teacher assessment!). The first part of the writing test consists of what is called the 'Shorter Task' and a spelling test. The Shorter Task has to be completed in 20 minutes, including five minutes' thinking time. The task booklet began with a writing prompt designed to help the pupils:

Endangered Creature
Imagine a creature called a Tongo Lizard.

It is an endangered creature, which means that very
few remain and it may become extinct.

[Picture of lizard.]

An information book about endangered creatures is
being prepared.

Your task is to write the page about the Tongo
Lizard.

This was followed by a planning format like a topic map and four prompts
for the children to think about. The mark scheme for the Shorter Task has
two components: 'sentence structure, punctuation and text organization'
are worth a maximum of four marks, and 'composition and effect' are
worth eight marks. When the seven marks for the spelling test are added
there is a total of 19 marks available for the short task.

The Longer Task had this prompt:

Dear Diary...
A brother and sister went on a day out with their family.

Tom really enjoyed the outing, but Sara did not.

[Picture of boy and girl with speech bubbles
expressing their different views.]

When they returned home, Tom and Sara wrote
about the day in their diaries.

Your task is to write Tom and Sara's diary entries.

The Longer Task has a maximum of eight marks for sentence structure
and punctuation, eight marks for text structure and organization, 12
marks for composition and effect, and three marks for handwriting. In
order to achieve the highest marks the criteria are:

Sentence structure and punctuation
Band A5
✪ *Length and focus of sentences varied to express*
subtleties in meaning and to focus on key ideas. Sentences

may include embedded subordinate clauses, sometimes
for economy of expression; word order used to create
emphasis/conversational effect. 8 marks

Text structure and organisation
Band B5
✪ *The structure of the text is controlled and shaped*
across the two diary entries. Sequencing of sections
or paragraphs contributes to overall effectiveness, e.g.
strategic placing of most significant event common to
both entries.
✪ *Sections or paragraphs varied in length and structure,*
ideas connected in a variety of ways, e.g. an event given
prominence in one diary is deliberately dealt with briefly
in the other. 8 marks

Composition and effect
Band C5
✪ *Choice and placing of content adapted for effect,*
e.g. contrast in characters subtly revealed by what is
prioritised or dealt with briefly.
✪ *Viewpoint well controlled and convincing, e.g. writer*
manages two contrasting positions and develops attitudes
of both characters through reflection.
✪ *Stylistic devices fully support purpose and engage, e.g.*
Tom's and Sara's language is stylistically distinct.
12 marks

Handwriting
Band F3
✪ *The handwriting is consistent and fluent with letters*
and words appropriately placed. The handwriting
maintains a personal style to engage the reader. 3 marks

One of the key features of the tests is that they are supposed to assess
your child's National Curriculum level for the different subj   The
average level for children's writing at the end of Key St

Level 4

Pupils' writing in a range of forms is lively and thoughtful. Ideas are often sustained and developed in interesting ways and organized appropriately for the purpose of the reader. Vocabulary choices are often adventurous and words are used for effect. Pupils are beginning to use grammatically complex sentences, extending meaning. Spelling, including that of polysyllabic words that conform to regular patterns, is generally accurate. Full stops, capital letters and question marks are used correctly, and pupils are beginning to use punctuation within the sentence. Handwriting style is fluent, joined and legible.

Some children will achieve Level 5:

Level 5

Pupils' writing is varied and interesting, conveying meaning clearly in a range of forms for different readers, using a more formal style where appropriate. Vocabulary choices are imaginative and words are used precisely. Simple and complex sentences are organized into paragraphs. Words with complex regular patterns are usually spelled correctly. A range of punctuation, including commas, apostrophes and inverted commas, is usually used accurately. Handwriting is joined, clear and fluent and, where appropriate, is adapted to a range of tasks.

To ensure that there is a match between these National Curriculum levels and the marking criteria for the tests, 'assessment focuses' are shown for the different marking categories shown above. So 'composition and effect' includes the assessment focus 'write imaginative, interesting and thoughtful texts', yet nowhere in the detail of the criteria is the marker required to make a judgement about whether the writing is 'imaginative' or 'ir_ere: i Nowhere! And therein lies the problem with the writing te_ the most important features about nearly every piece of writing is that it is interesting. For fiction and poetry, in particular, the imagination of the writer is absolutely central to the success of the writing. Given that both the short test and the long test required the children to 'Use your imagination', it is doubly remiss that the criteria did not require the markers to make a judgement about this.

Which of the following two pieces of writing do you like best?

I had an awful day...we went to a Roman museum, I've always wanted to go there. Oh, how could you tell I was being sarcastic? It was so boring. I begged and pleaded not to go right from the beginning. My feet hurt where we trampled round every tiny inch of the museum. I decided to cheer myself up by helping Tom build the tapestry but it just got me down even more because it was far too hard, but Tom managed to do it and he's younger than me! By the time we got to write our name in Roman I was bored stiff. What a stupid idea it was to write our name in Roman. Only people from sadland would do that! Oh, to make matters worse we stopped at every single fact sheet, and there were 200 of them. I was tired, bored and just over all FED UP! I mean we must have been the first family to stand there and look at every single fact sheet. I hope we never go back there again.

I had an awful day...my little brother threw sand at me. My dad threw me under the water. My mum pulled my hair and when I had an ice-cream my brother made me drop it so that I couldn't have one. The best bit was when we had lunch because I had more than my brother. But when we went on the jet skis I fell off and nearly drowned. Then we went home we fell asleep in the car. When we woke up my brother came over and gave me a cuddle and he brought me an ice-cream with his money. My mum took me out shopping with my friends and I got 2 dresses and 2 tops.

There are many things about the second piece that I like. The images are instantly recognizable, powerful and presented in quick succession. This is a writer using their senses and their authentic memories of childhood: sand in the eyes; struggling to breathe underwater; the disappointment of the upturned ice-cream, and the real danger of drowning. And what a wonderful touching moment when the brother gives his sister a cuddle – read Anthony Browne's book *Tunnel* for a powerful exploration of these emotions. It's a shame that the repetition of 'when/then we' wasn't varied more towards the end of the piece.

The writer of the first piece does use devices well, and I liked the idea of 'sadland' particularly. But, just as the writer was bored, well I'm afraid I got bored reading about them being bored. It also made me want to say, you ungrateful child you don't deserve to be taken to a museum! But perhaps that is a sign that the writer had engaged my emotions. You may have felt differently about the two pieces of writing.

And the marks for these pieces of writing for composition and effect, shown in the test marking guide for 2006? – 12 marks for the first piece and **three marks** for the second piece.

Try looking at it this way

To finish this chapter, and the book, I want to remind you of Esther's piece of writing about the Tooth Fairy that you looked at as part of Chapter 5. My thoughts about her writing caused me to question the criteria for the National Tests. The test criteria at Key Stage 1 fail to reward creativity and imagination adequately, just as the criteria at Key Stage 2 do. So I decided to write some different criteria. These are the ones that I think you should judge your child's writing by when you look at it at home:

✪ How much *originality* is represented through *choice* and selection of ideas?

✪ How are real-life and textual *influences* used?

✪ How much *thought* does the writing engender in readers?

✪ How *playful* is the writer?

✪ What kind of *emotional* response does the writing engender?

✪ What was the nature of thought *during* the process of writing?

If we can't abolish the tests altogether, we could have them replaced by teacher assessment only. Teachers are in a position to assess the kinds of things in my list. More importantly, if you respond to your child's writing by talking about these things, then you will be laying the foundations for greater success than any test can show.

Expectations for a child's writing at age 11

What you can expect	What you can do to help
Using information sources and writing to learn.	Support the skills of note-taking and/or tabulating information, etc.
Will redraft composition as well as transcription elements.	Help your child to see the value of redrafting to improve the final product. Support their proof-reading skills.
Able to successfully control a range of text forms and has developed expertise in favourites.	Encourage experimentation to find types of writing that they enjoy.
Length of writing increasing.	Help your child to control the larger structural elements, such as headings and paragraphs.
Growing understanding of levels of formality in writing.	Discuss differences between things like emails to friends and family as opposed to formal letters.
Standard spelling most of the time. Efficient use of dictionaries and spell-checks.	Help your child to enjoy the wealth of information contained in dictionaries. Show them how to use standard adult dictionaries.
Basic punctuation secure. Aware of a range of other marks.	Encourage use of full range of punctuation. Enjoy spotting things like the 'grocer's apostrophe'.
Presentation and fluency of handwriting differentiated for purpose.	Support handwriting with good-quality pens and other implements. Encourage proper typing when using computer keyboard.

Further help

I'm very interested to hear about your experiences using the ideas in this book with your children. Feel free to send me examples of things that you've done, or questions and queries, and I will do my very best to answer. Please put 'Parents' in the email subject box and contact me at bdw28@cam.ac.uk. Now, here are some useful websites:

Government's Parents Centre: parentscentre.gov.uk/
A mass of information for parents, including useful stuff about reading and writing. Neglects possibilities for mark-making for children under three.

Bookstart: bookstart.co.uk/bookstart/index.php4
Information about how you can get a pack of free books for your child and some guidance on using them.

BBC Parenting site: bbc.co.uk/parenting/
A wealth of information.

Direct.Gov: direct.gov.uk/EducationAndLearning/fs/en
Gives information about public services. Basic advice about reading is included.

The Basic Skills Agency: basic-skills.co.uk/
This is a useful site which includes some information about Story Sacks.

A Story Sack is a large cloth bag containing a good-quality children's picture book with supporting materials to stimulate a wide range of language, literacy and numeracy activities. It contains soft toys of the main characters with props and scenery relating to the story to bring the book to life. The Sack also contains a non-fiction book drawing out one of the story's themes, a language- or number-based game to enhance specific skills and ideas for things to do. Included in the Sack is an audio tape, enabling parents to share the story without needing to read it.

Story Sacks are an enjoyable way to share books and bring them to life. The aim of a Story Sack is to give parents confidence to enjoy books and reading with their child. Not every parent finds it easy to read stories, but Story Sacks offer supporting materials to help parents share books with their child. (Basic Skills Agency [2006], accessed 30 March, 2006.)

References

Before you start this book

1 Durkin, D. (1966). *Children Who Read Early*. New York: Teachers College Press

2 Clarke, M. M. (1967). *Young Fluent Readers: What can they teach us?* London: Heinemann Educational.

Chapter 1

1 Opie, I. and Opie, P. (1951). *The Oxford Dictionary of Nursery Rhymes*. Oxford: Oxford University Press, p.364.

2 Opie, I. and Opie, P. (1951) p.363.

3 Ziegler, J., and Goswami, U. (2005). 'Reading acquisition, developmental dyslexia and skilled reading across languages; a psycholinguistic grain size theory'. *Psychological Bulletin, 131(1)*, 3–29.

4 Taylor, K. (2004, October 22). 'Eat your heart out'. *Guardian Unlimited*.

5 Holdaway, D. (1979). *The Foundations of Literacy*. London: Ashton Scholastic.

6 Arizpe, E., and Styles, M. (2003). *Children Reading Pictures: Interpreting visual texts*. London: RoutledgeFalmer.

7 Arizpe and Styles. p.57.

8 Arizpe and Styles. p.224.

9 Clay, M. (1979). *The Early Detection of Reading Difficulties* (3rd ed.). Auckland: New Zealand: Heinemann Education.

Chapter 2

1 Cooke, T., and Oxenbury, H. (1996). *So Much*. London: Walker Books Ltd.
2 Oakley, H. (1988). *On My Bike*. Aylesbury: Ginn.

3 Moon, C. (2006). *Individualised Reading 2006*. Readi Reading.

4 Goswami, U. (2005). 'Synthetic phonics and learning to read: A cross-language perspective'. *Educational Psychology in Practice, 21*(4), 273–282.

5 Goswami, U. (2005), p.275 (adapted from Seymour, Aro and Erskine, 2003).

Chapter 3

1 Almond, D. (1998). *Skellig*. London: Hodder Children's Books.

2 Almond, D. (1998), p.168

3 Beard, G., and Hutchins, H. (2002). *The Adventures of Super Diaper Baby*. London: Scholastic.

4 Beard, G., and Hutchins, H. (2002), p.77, 79, 76.

5 Hahn, D., Flynn, L., and Reuben, S. (eds.) (2004). *The Ultimate Book Guide*. London: A & C Black.

6 Wyse, D. and Jones, R. (2001). *Teaching, English, Language and Literacy*. London: RoutledgeFalmer.

7 Gorard, S. (2006). 'Value-added is of little value'. *Journal of Educational Policy, 21(2)*, 235–243.

8 Boyle, B., and Bragg, J. (2006). 'A curriculum without foundation'. *British Educational Research Journal, 32(4)*, 569–582.

Chapter 4

1 Harste, J. C., Woodward, V. A., & Burke, C. L. (1984). *Language Stories & Literacy Lessons*. Portsmouth, NH: Heinemann Educational Books.

2 Sassoon, R. (2003). *Handwriting: The way to teach it* (2nd ed.) London: Paul Chapman Publishing.

3 Jarman, C. (1979). *The Development of Handwriting Skills: A resource book for teachers*. Oxford: Basil Blackwell.

4 Barber, C. (1993). *The English Language: A historical introduction*. Cambridge: Cambridge University Press.

5 Pyles, T., and Algeo, J. (1993). *The Origins and Development of the English Language* London: Harcourt Brace Jovanovich, p.286.

Cambridge Encyclopedia of Language (2nd ed.). University Press.

7 Bryson, B. (1990). *Mother Tongue. The English language.* London: Penguin Books. p.57

8 Crystal, D. (2004). *The Stories of English.* London: Penguin/Allen Lane.

9 Greenbaum, S. (1986). 'Spelling variants in British English'. *Journal of English Linguistics, 19,* 258–68.

10 Gentry, R. (1982). 'An analysis of developmental spelling in gnys at wrk'. *Reading Teacher, 36,* 192–200.

11 Bissex, G. (1980). *GNYS AT WRK: A child learns to read and write.* Cambridge, Massachusetts: Harvard University Press.

12 Hall, N., and Robinson, A. (eds.) (1996). *Learning About Punctuation.* Clevedon: Multilingual Matters.

Chapter 5

1 Crystal, D. (2004). *Rediscover Grammar* (3rd ed.). Harlow: Pearson Education.

2 Carter, R., and McCarthy, M. (2006). *Cambridge Grammar of English.* Cambridge: Cambridge University Press.

3 Truss, L. (2003). *Eats, Shoots and Leaves: The zero tolerance approach to punctuation.* London: Profile Books.

4 Sassoon, R. (2003). *Handwriting: The way to teach it* (2nd ed.). London: Paul Chapman Publishing.

Chapter 6

1 Martin, J., Christie, F., and Rothery, J. (1987). 'Social processes in education: A reply to Sawayer and Watson (and others)'. In I. Reid (ed.), *The Place of Genre in Learning.* Victoria: Deakin University.

2 Wray, D., and Medwell, J. (1997). *QTS English for Primary Teachers.* London: Letts.

3 Salda, M. (2005). The Little Red Riding Hood Project. Retrieved 4 August 2006 from usm.edu/english/fairytales/lrrh/lrrhhome.htm

4 Wray, D., and Lewis, M. (1997). *Extending Literacy: Children reading and writing non-fiction.* London: Routledge, p.53.

5 Lewis, M., and Wray, D. (1995). *Developing Children's Non-fiction Writing: Working with writing frames.* Leamington Spa: Scholastic, p.85.

6 Jaffrey, M. (1982). *Madhur Jaffrey's Indian Cookery.* London: BBC Publications, p.75.

7 Rhodes, G. (1994). *Rhodes Around Britain.* London: BBC Publications, p.62.

8 Joyce, J. (1922). *Ulysses.* First published in its entirety, Paris: Sylvia Beach, p.608

9 McCourt, F. (1996). *Angela's Ashes.* London: HarperCollins, p.7.

10 Oakley, H. (1988). *On My Bike.* Aylesbury: Ginn.

11 Waugh, D. (1998). 'Practical approaches to teaching punctuation in the primary school'. *Reading, 32(2),* 14–17.

Picture Credits

Acknowledgements

Text and image from *Where is my home? A Sunshine Garden Activity Book* is reproduced by permission of Boots Company PLC

The Very Hungry Caterpillar by Eric Carle. Copyright ©1969 and 1987 by Eric Carle. All rights reserved. Image reproduced with permission.

Extract and images from *Lily Takes A Walk* by Satoshi Kitamura (Blackie 1990) Copyright © Satoshi Kitamura, 1987, reproduced by permission of Penguin Group

Cover of *Willie the Wizard* reprinted by permission of The Random House Group Limited

Cover of *Teletubbies and the Flying Toast*, BBC Books, reprinted by permission of Ragdoll

Text © 1994 Trish Cooke
Extract from *So Much* by Trish Cooke and illustrated by Helen Oxenbury Reproduced by permission of Walker Books Ltd, London SE11 5HJ

Copyright © 1990 Lucy Cousins
Lucy Cousins font © 1990 Lucy Cousins
Illustration from *Maisy Goes to Bed* by Lucy Cousins
Maisy™. Maisy is a registered trademark of Walker Books Ltd
Reproduced by permissions of Walker Books Ltd, London SE11 5HJ

Extract from *Skellig* © David Almond, reprinted by kind permission of the author

Extract from Hahn, D., Flynn, L., & Reuben, S. (Eds.). (2004). *The Ultimate Book Guide*. London: A & C Black, reproduced by permission of A & C Black

Extracts from *QCA KS2 National Tests: English 2006 (Reading test)* and *QCA KS2 Tests: English 2006 (Writing test)* reproduced by permission of QCA Enterprises

Extract from *Mother Tongue: The English Language* by Bill Bryson (Hamish Hamilton, 1990) Copyright © Bill Bryson, 1990, reproduced by permission of Penguin Group

Figure 4.4 from Jarman, C. (1979). *The development of handwriting skills: A resource book for teachers* is reprinted by permission of Oxford: Basil Blackwell.